A Time for Memories

With Best Wishes

Molly Bihet.

A Time for Memories

Molly Bihet

AMBERLEY

First published 2005 by Molly Bihet

This edition published 2009

Amberley Publishing Plc
Cirencester Road, Chalford
Stroud, Gloucestershire, GL6 8PE

www.amberley-books.com

British Library Cataloguing in Publication Data.
A catalogue record for this book is available from the British Library.

ISBN 978 1 84868 207 8

Typesetting and origination by Amberley Publishing
Printed and bound in Great Britain

Contents

The German Occupation
of a Part of the British Empire

On June 28, 1940, Goering sent a handful of bombers to the Channel Islands. Guernsey lost 34 people and Jersey 10.

Two days later the Nazis landed at Guernsey Airport. A message was flashed to the Military Governor of occupied Paris who telephoned Field Marshall Keital who notified Hitler

The Führer told his aides: "Now we have our foot inside the door of the British Empire!"

At his secret daily conference on July 3rd, Dr. Goebbels ordered the German Press never to use the term "British Empire."

Roosevelt and Stalin knew the Islands had fallen, Churchill was uncertain. On July 3 he wrote to General Ismay: "If it be true that German troops have landed on Jersey and Guernsey . . ."

Preface

THE FIVE LONG OCCUPATION YEARS

It is 20 years since I wrote *A Child's War* and over 10 years sitting and reliving my life and having more Occupation stories in *Reflections of Guernsey*. I always felt that some day there would be a third book.

As we celebrate the Liberation of Guernsey, the Islands and the 60 years of freedom, we remember the great joy of receiving the Red Cross messages sent and received between December 1940 and May 1945. Also the wonderful food parcels plus other commodities that came monthly from The Red Cross between December 1944 and June 5th 1945.

From June 1944 and the D-Day Landing, Islands were literally cut off and no food and commodities could be shipped from France to us. During the last six months of the German Occupation, many of the population were indeed starving and in a very poor way. But for the arrival of the *Vega*, many more hundreds would have died. The parcels of food were indeed a godsend.

Relive those days by reading personal accounts by the late 'Dame of Sark', Mrs Sibyl Hathaway, who was greatly respected and who worked hard throughout to ease any situation that arose in the Island of Sark and always thought of the well-being of the Sarkees. Frank, christened Francis, a Guernseyman and Hedy Collenette, were a couple who married in 1938. Frank recounts the difficulties they faced during the Occupation of Guernsey. Frank worked for the Germans, mainly at the airport and tells of happenings to himself and of his friends and family.

There are also tales and stories (some funny and some frightening) by four young single Guernseymen, who also worked or were working alongside the forces.

Bill Gillingham who kindly wrote his recollections for me and other interesting stories from Alf Le Poidevin, Bill Martel and Alf Williams.

A big coincidence came by still living at Woodcote, our home for some 30 years, and meeting with Helmut Methner in 1999.

There are copies and stories behind the Red Cross letters and the appreciation and the arrival of the *Vega*, bringing us food parcels. What a celebration and relief!

Before the arrival of this special boat, you may be interested to read of Occupation recipes and how the housewives had to substitute then.

To conclude, Veterans of Force 135 tells of the emotions felt remembering our liberation time in 1945 and of the celebrations after 50 years of Freedom in 1995.

My memories will include the 40th, 50th and the 60 years of Liberation and its celebrations.

The special years that will no doubt always be remembered in our Guernsey history for the future.

Molly Bihet

Acknowledgements

My very special thanks to our daughter, Sally Howlett, who has given her time and patience typing my longhand. To Sue Attewell, her friend of many years and to Keith Matthews, another friend – a big thank you also for your typing skills and helping me out.

Not forgetting also a special thank you to my husband, André, who at last can sit down to a meal without volumes of paper surrounding him!

I have been very fortunate as so many have given me their time and trusted me with their precious Red Cross messages and photographs. They have been helpful in so many different ways and I have been very grateful to one and all.

Sincere thanks also to:

Miss Caroline Bell
Miss Heidi Collenette
Mr Bill Gillingham
Mr Alf Williams
Mrs Ann Wilkes-Green
Mr Robert (Bob) Brown
Mrs Shiela Brown
Mr Jim Priaulx
Mr Richard Heaume
Mr John Goodwin
Mr Bill Bell
Major Evan Ozanne
Mr Neville Robilliard
Mrs Madeleine Sims
Mrs Elizabeth Orr
Mr Donald Smith

Mrs Hazel Tomlinson
Miss Mary Sims
Mr John Salmon
Mrs Dorothy Dowding
Mrs Marion Petit
Mrs Rhona Moriarty
Mrs Emmie Taylor
Mrs Rosemary McClean
Mrs Barbara Stoney
Mr Ken Bonsall
Mr Lloyd Le Prevost
Mrs Pat Foley
Mr David Pattimore
Mrs Karen Taylor
Mrs Thelma Bennett
The Staff at J. H. Haynes

Sibyl Hathaway, 12th May 1945, with her French poodles Bella and Beau

PART ONE

Mrs Sibyl Hathaway
La Dame de Sark

At the beginning of the conflict, Mrs Hathaway never thought for one minute that Sark, her peaceful Island, would be touched by war.

Sark was looking forward to holiday visitors during the early part of 1940 and travel agents were suggesting the Channel Islands as an 'ideal' holiday destination away from the war.

As German troops advanced towards the French coast and listening to the news at La Seigneurie, the home of the Dame and her husband, Robert (Bob) realised that maybe Sark could be liable to an attack, with the other Channel Islands.

She happened to be in Guernsey during the evacuation and naturally being concerned, decided with her husband to hold a meeting with Sark residents on the 23rd June, on her return to the Island.

It was a peaceful evening meeting and Dame Sibyl reassured the population that should the Germans arrive in Sark, she would deal with them as she thought best and wanted to encourage everyone to stay in their homes. She was a strong character and with her last forceful words 'Britain will win – Britain will win', everyone cheered loudly and the outcome of her persuasion was that 471 people remained. Most of the English residents had already left.

The first meeting with the Germans was with Guernsey's first Commandant, Major Albrecht Lanz and a Doctor Maas, his Chief of Staff. This meeting gave the Dame and her husband great satisfaction as they felt they had succeeded in gaining respect from them – as before entering the Seigneurie drawing room where Dame Sybil and Robert were sitting at the far end of a large solid oak writing table, the German Officials asked Cecile (who worked at the Seigneurie) for a brush to clean their boots after carefully wiping their feet on the doormat! Sitting dignified, the Dame had wanted them to have to walk to where she and Bob were sitting and she felt she had gained respect for the house from them.

Dame Sibyl, because of her fluent knowledge of German, gained respect not only from the Germans but also from the Sark population, always doing her best for them, especially taking an interest in the schools and the children's welfare ensuring they were adequately clothed and fed.

I have felt privileged and have been so very grateful to Miss Caroline Bell, Dame Sibyl's granddaughter, who has allowed me to read all of the Dame's letters and correspondence and those of her husband (see later) from during the Occupation.

Dame Sibyl died in 1974 at the age of 90 years.

This is Dame Sibyl's account of the Occupation, in her own words, which I know you will find very interesting.

- DAME SYBIL'S STORY -

During June 1940 when daily arrivals of fishing boats full of refugees from France came in to collect fresh water and food and tell us of the horrors of invasion, it became apparent to us that it could not be long before we were to suffer the same fate. Fortunately for the lives and property of the people of these thickly populated Islands, the British Government decided it was impracticable to attempt or defend them. With the French Airfields so nearby and masses of artillery, it would have meant devastation for us, so we were all faced with deciding whether to go to England as refugees in the many ships provided for the Islanders by the British Government, or to stay by their property and homes and hope for the best.

Left to right: *Kratzer, Roeffler, Bob Hathaway, Lanz – Commandant of the Channel Islands, Schumacher, J. Tetley, Maas, Von Stein. Sark, 1940*

In spite of many telegrams from family and friends both in England and the USA my husband and I felt we had no alternative but to remain and accept the responsibility it entailed. I called a meeting of the inhabitants and told them of our decision and advised all who had a home and stake in the land to remain. I urged men of military age to go and I advised that families should not be broken up, if the children were to be sent away at least one of the parents should be with them.

I warned of the likely scarcity of food, but I added we would always have cows and fish and rabbits. I am thankful that at the time I had no idea of the five weary years ahead and the difficulties over even those seemingly plentiful commodities. The result of this meeting was that no Sark-born person left the Island, a certain number of our English residents left, and the doctor.

Though the Island was completely de-militarised by the 28th June, on that day the Germans attacked the harbour of St Peter Port from the air, machine gunning and killing some 30 people, and they flew low over the sea between Guernsey and Sark. They fired at our small fishing boats around the coast, luckily they escaped. The next day the Germans landed on the Guernsey Airport and took control of that Island. Our telephone was cut and for four days we knew nothing about what was happening in Guernsey. No boats dared to put out after their recent experience so we had to wait in the greatest suspense for our fate to be made known to us. At last, on July 3rd we saw the old Guernsey lifeboat heading for Sark. (At that time the Germans had brought no boats at all).

Having been to the school and reassured the children and some of the women who had read of German brutalities in Poland, I sent the Seneschal to the Harbour to meet them and bring them to the Seigneurie. My husband and I sat in the drawing room and waited. I tried to take a leaf out of Mussolini's book and sat at the far end of a long room – behind a desk!

When they arrived I heard them wiping their feet on the door mat, a most reassuring gesture of respect to the house. Of course I expected to hear 'Heil Hitler' when they entered the room, but I must say here and now, that never once was it said in my presence in the five years of occupation. Only three officers came in, with the Nazi salute, the Commanding Officer, Lanz indicated a Naval Captain Maas as interpreter, but as I had lived in Germany after the 1914 war long enough to know enough of the language to carry on conversation I spoke in German. A large printed order was produced, the usual restrictions about arms, no assembling of more than five people in public – no God Save the King and all licensed premises to be closed, and of course a curfew at 9pm. We were allowed to keep our radios and cameras until the following year.

The occupation of the Channel Islands by the Germans could have no possible effect on the outcome of the war; they were so anxious for propaganda purposes to hold British land that they were prepared to isolate numbers of men and use such material for this. At this time they were winning the war everywhere, and as usual with them, they had an intense desire to make a good impression where people of what they called Kultur were concerned. They assured us that the war would be over by Christmas, and went so far as to buy up all the tweeds in Guernsey which they assured us were to be made into suits for them in London. They also said they would now invade England if it meant losing a million men and almost laughed when we showed signs of doubt about that venture.

We found out afterwards that the first invaders had been specially picked, on purpose to show British people what good fellows the Germans really were. At first, it was entirely a military occupation, on the 4th July a Sergeant and ten men took over the so-called military control of the Island. As it was American Independence Day, my husband, American-born and an old Yale man, remarked that that was a 'hell of a date to be taken over by the Huns'. The first few months

of occupation were quiet and uneventful. I was told to carry on all civil administration as usual and in any difficulties to send direct complaint to the officer
commanding the Forces, who was in Guernsey. This proved the strongest string
in my hand. All through the Occupation I acted on this and always went over the
heads of all others direct to him, and found that, with the strict discipline in the
army, his was a marvellous deterrent to any petty tyranny by local officers.

Our quiet existence began to change – about December 1940. We had been
warned that the military authorities would turn over their administration to civil
officials and then conditions for us would deteriorate. The stage was now set for
this, swarms of officials in all varieties of uniforms came over and demanded sta-
tistics of every conceivable kind. This became an epidemic and one had to be ready
with details of all sorts at a moment's notice. Financially they were most assidu-
ous, demanding constant balance sheets of the Island finance, which must include
an 'estimate of future revenue'. As we were then paying the cost of maintaining the
troops in the Island, and their numbers varied from week to week, the estimates
were quite worthless. I must say they never criticised or verified our figures until
the last six months of the war when our 11 months' siege became a grave anxiety
to them.

Of all the Islands we were in the best position to withstand the Occupation.
We had no town population to feed. We were some 471 people mostly able to
produce some vegetables, a few rabbits and some had cows and pigs, and many
were fishermen.

A Murder In Sark

Early in 1941 we had our first taste of the Gestapo. The German doctor in charge
of the troops was found one morning murdered in his bed, and of course they were
determined to try and fix the crime on to a Sark person. The doctor's batman was
missing, news of this soon got around to us and we were accused of harbouring
him. A curfew was imposed at 7pm – this in May and with the wartime two hour
early Summer Time, so that actually we were shut in from a daylight point of view,
at 5pm! A special permit had to be got from the German Commandant to allow
a man to attend to his cattle after that hour. For 10 days the batman could not be
found, and every male from sixteen to seventy-years-old had to report twice a day
at the Kommandantur. It was then discovered that the batman's body was in the
bottom of the well at the doctor's house, so suspicion was rather grudgingly lifted
from Sark men. The man was buried in a desolate spot on the cliff in the dead of
night and we heard nothing more of the matter.

I only left the Island once during the whole of the Occupation, as I was afraid of
what requisitions might be made in my absence if I were not there to argue about
them. On this one occasion, I had to go because word was brought secretly to me
that two British Officers had landed from a submarine and were in hiding in my
daughter's empty house in Guernsey. The man left in charge of the place came over
to me as he had no means of helping them, having no ration cards they had no chance
of getting food. I took some tinned supplies and went across to Guernsey, making
a cautious visit to the house on the pretext of being in charge of my daughter's

property I found two young officers of my son-in-law's regiment. It seemed that the submarine which should have come to take them off must have been lost in the Channel, so they had no means of getting away. They hoped I could get a fishing boat from Sark, but these were so strictly guarded by the Germans that it was quite impossible – also a difficulty in getting enough petrol. In the end they had to give themselves up and were taken to prison in Germany. The sad thing was that members of their families living in Guernsey were deported to France, though they were completely innocent – as a punishment of a typically Nazi kind.

The costs of the Occupation were now falling heavily on the finances of the Island. The Germans had said that they would pay two-thirds of these, but of course they never did, and even if they had done so it would have been in their specially printed Occupation marks, which they valued a 2 shillings and 1 penny and which we knew had no real value.

About this time my eldest son was killed in the Liverpool Blitz. He was in the RAF but was actually on leave, and in a hotel at the time. My daughter asked at the American Embassy if they could get the news to me, as the United States was at yet not in the war. A message was sent via the Berlin Consulate to the Commandant in Guernsey, then General von Schmettow, to transmit to me, and I must say he showed the greatest kindness and consideration in doing so with as little shock to me as possible. Our telephones had by then all been taken away from us so a message was brought to my husband to go to the Sark Commandant's office, and there he was told the news and asked to break it to me. I felt that this was kindly of the General but the strangest thing was, that a few days later he and his A.D.C. came to pay a call and express their condolences. It was quite one of the most difficult moments for me, to calmly accept this from the enemy but he wisely said that his sympathy was for all mothers who all grieved in the same way in every nation for their sons.

Two years later his own son was killed in Russia and feeling that I must uphold the tradition of British courtesy in the same way, I sent him a card of sympathy.

ANNOYING THE GERMANS

Now I must try and say a little about the psychology of occupier and occupied and the strain of keeping the balance between them. In the first place we could do no good in any way by any sabotage, there could be no underground movement where there was absolutely no contact with outside. We were like prisoners in a jail with a garden to it! Our only weapon was propaganda, always keeping cheerfully confident of victory for the Allies, never disagreeing openly but asking ostensibly silly questions such as 'Haven't you landed in England yet?', or 'I suppose Russia has now been conquered'. Our wireless sets had all been taken away as a supposed reprisal for the escape of some men from Guernsey in a small fishing boat.

Another way I found I could annoy was to ask about education in Germany and when told of their Hitler Youth Camps, express great surprise that people would allow their children to be sent to these against the parents' wishes. I stressed that we had our own ideas on education in England and were free to choose schools

'The White Heather' of Sark in Creux Harbour, Sark (under guard)

for our children. I found that this particularly stung the fathers who were Roman Catholic. I had of course practically no contacts except with the Commandants or the doctors, the former was never allowed to visit us without some staff to spy on him – but the doctors were different. We were entirely without a doctor, ours having left when the Occupation was imminent, so I got a District Nurse over from Guernsey with her husband and carried on until she herself had twins whom I had to help into the world myself. After that I appealed for medical help to the General, who at that time was Prince Oettingen, a charming man with whom I had numerous mutual friends. He later suffered a lot from the Nazi regime and his daughter-in-law was imprisoned by Hitler. He came over to see me and at once promised to send the Oberstabsartz to arrange with me about medical aid, which from time to time was given willingly and unstintedly at any hour by the army doctor stationed in Sark. These doctors were changed every two months as they were always suspected of being too much influenced by the Islanders!

Needless to say I had a hidden wireless set and there was one other on the Island. The penalty if discovered was 30,000 marks, which of course no one had, or imprisonment, or in certain cases, death. We hid our set in a trunk left behind by one of our friends who evacuated; in fact, I had a stack of trunks and suitcases of other peoples' in an empty room, so this one among the pile did not arouse any suspicion when they searched the house as they sometimes did. I went to the length of packing it in an old moth-eaten blanket to which we added moths from time to time. We only dared listen in at 9pm, just my husband and I and our farm bailiff and his wife. We had a sort of drill as to what to do if the Germans were suddenly to come to the front or back door. I had two large poodles who were ready to bark at any sound, which would warn us. I was to go slowly to the door making a fuss of quietening the dogs while the others were putting away the set. It was risky but we could not stand being in complete ignorance of the real things happening all over the world, and kept our sanity in spite of bad news and constant German propaganda by the troops and their newspapers.

All our thoughts and conversation began to be about food. I still remember the intense relief every Saturday of having got through one more week. We had masses of lobsters but found nothing to use to vary the ways of cooking them. The same of rabbits. We began to run out of many things; sugar, tea, coffee, tobacco. At first there was a purchasing commission of representatives who went under a German escort to France to buy necessities. Our staunch friend was Mr. R.O. Falla from Guernsey who always helped our needs, especially for agriculture. Things began to get short in France, and everything had to be paid for in Occupation marks.

If anything could be called amusing at this time it was the German effort to control our fishing. They were so afraid of the possible escape of a fishing boat which might reach England that an armed German soldier was placed in each boat, in spite of the fact that no boat had enough petrol to reach England. Then the disciplined German mind proceeded to fix the time of day for fishing, completely ignoring the variation of tides, the one essential condition for a successful catch. For instance, they would affix a notice saying 'Fishing tomorrow will be allowed between 10am and 3pm', the guards would be waiting at the harbour but no fisherman, who knew that at 10am it would be useless to fish and waste some of their petrol which was extremely precious and by now strictly rationed. The guards reported their absence to the local Commandant who always came to me to complain. Explanations and a promise on his part to 'appeal higher authority' to have the hours varied. Whoever his higher authority may have been, it took some time to get it understood that hours as such had nothing to do with fishing – in the end it was realised that tides mattered, especially as the Germans needed fish as much as we did. The fishermen got much amusement out of the often sea-sick guards in their boats and more than one German got well soaked by being deliberately steered into quite avoidable large waves.

DEPORTATION BRINGS A TRAGEDY

The situation seemed quiet, when out of the blue, in September 1942, an order came that all British residents in Sark, as distinct from actual Island born, were to be evacuated to Germany. Only 11 people were ordered to assemble at the harbour in four days' time to board a boat for France. By now of course, on our secret radio sets, we had got to know of all the vile things being done by the Germans, in the countries they had occupied, but it was a shock to us after the almost mild subjection in which we lived. One middle-aged English couple faced the news of their order to go, in a tragic state of panic, which led to the nearest escape I had of being involved by the Gestapo. This couple decided to die rather than go, and on the morning of the day of departure, they could not be found. Their farm manager came to my husband to ask if they were in our house, but the previous day we had only seen them for a few moments when they came to ask me to take charge of three letters and her jewellery, which they explained in a perfectly normal way they did not wish to leave in an empty house. I went to the harbour with packets of sandwiches etc. for the journey of those leaving, and when after a long wait these people did not turn up I had to tell the local Commandant that I feared something was wrong. He dashed off in the car they had brought over to Sark for the use of officers, and after another miserable half-hour of waiting for the remaining nine people to be deported, the boat was ordered to leave. I got to the house of the missing couple as soon as ever I could but only to find it full of Germans, and entrance was forbidden. That evening they searched all our houses for traces of them, but of course no one had seen them. At a very early hour I was awakened by a German outside my windows asking me to come at once to the house as they had found our friend, and she was begging for me to come. I got there very quickly and found he was dead and she was in a terrible state, having stabbed herself in 16 places. I must say now that the German doctor and the Commandant were exceedingly helpful and laid on their ambulance and boat and allowed me to telephone to Guernsey for her to be taken to the civil hospital there. Luckily for her that she contracted pneumonia and was too ill for weeks to be bullied or cross-questioned but it was not so easy for me, as unfortunately they had left a letter addressed to me, that I knew nothing about. I had a very unpleasant time with the Gestapo cross-questioning me all one morning. There were determined that there must be some mystery about this Major Sxxxx and tried in every way to prove that he was some sort of British Agent. After they left I felt in my bones that they would come back unexpectedly and search because they kept repeating the question: 'Have you any documents or papers?' – so I hastily hid the three letters I had under the straw in my rabbit hutches, when sure enough they came back and persisted in their questions. I had told them only that I had the jewellery. Suddenly the most aggressive of them produced a letter which he thrust at me, pointing to the words: 'You have our last messages'. I took a long breath while he asked: 'What is the meaning of that?' The word 'meaning' gave me my cue and I firmly said that in English messages meant words spoken not written! And the messages I had were only connected with the jewellery and to whom it was to be sent if they did not return. Somehow I got away with it and heard no more about it but it was a difficult moment as I had no idea that Major Sxxxx had left a letter of farewell addressed to me. I was able to send the letters safely to their addresses after our Liberation.

ENGLISH COMMANDO RAID AND A KILLING

Our garrison varied in numbers. We could only guess at the total. They took over all hotels and houses that had been vacated by evacuating summer residents, but it was not until after the first English Commando raid on the Island that they moved all their troops to the centre of the Island and surrounded themselves with barbed wire. This raid took place one night at the end of September. It was led by Major Geoffrey Appleyard with a Lieutenant Pinckney and the Norwegian VC Anders Lassen, who was also a triple MC. They landed about midnight at the foot of a steep cliff known as the Hogs Back. Appleyard had spent several holidays in Sark and knew it well. He led the party across the valley and up to a house that seemed empty. They broke a window and prepared to rush the house when they were greeted by a woman who thought the house must be on fire! She had a shock at seeing their black faces but realised they were British and prepared to give any help. Her husband, Dr. Pittard, had died some months earlier and she was alone

Bob and Sibyl outside La Seigneurie

in the house. She gave all the information she could about the recent deportations, and put them wise about the Germans occupying part of the nearby Dixcart Hotel. After killing one German they took three others prisoner, but when these saw how few the British were they started to resist and make an outcry. A real struggle began – one more German was killed and they started to take the other two away to the boat when one escaped. Their hands had been tied when they struggled and resisted and the one who escaped took news of this to the rest of the Germans who by now were all aroused and shooting and shouting. However, they reached the boat safely and got under way.

Next day, the German propaganda condemned the illegal tying of the prisoners' hands and in a speech in Edinburgh the following week, Mr. Churchill announced that the Germans had shackled the hands of all British prisoners as a reprisal, so this Sark raid had terrible repercussions.

The Germans noticed the broken window at Mrs. Pittard's house and traced footprints and although she protested that she had not been to blame, she was abruptly removed to the prison in Guernsey and afterwards to Germany until the end of the war.

After this raid, things were much harder for us. More wire than ever was put up and over 13,000 land mines were laid all on land at the top of the cliffs, in many cases in some of our best agricultural land. The rabbits bred in these minefields and came out at night and ate all our crops. The Germans stole all our snares so that we could not catch any to eat ourselves.

In February 1943, orders came for some sixty-three more people to be deported. These ranged from children aged eight years to people up to sixty-six years. We were told that the order for this came from the 'highest command'. We never discovered the reason for this deportation. We were then only 363 persons in the

Island. After the war I enquired the reason of Prince Oettingen, who told me he had never understood it and had protested against it and got into trouble for doing so, and finally was removed from his command in Guernsey for daring to protest.

My husband was among those taken. I was told it was because all men who had held a commission were to be taken and they had found out that he had been an officer in the Royal Flying Corps in the 1914 war. He was then a young man in New York and pretended to be a Canadian, and like many of his friends enlisted in the British Flying Corps as the RAF was then known. It was an order that all retired British officers were to be taken to Germany up to the age of seventy, but it did not make sense to us to take women and children of all ages, even aged sixty-five to seventy and send them packed in boat and train to misery in Germany for 2½ years. The boats were perfectly awful and the conditions in which the women and children were herded at xxxx Race Course in Paris in make-shift quarters in the Grand Stand.

LETTERS TO BOB – FUEL, FOOD AND CLOTHES

My husband was taken to Laufen, an old Schloss built for the Bishops of Salzburg in the Middle Ages. The walls were full of bugs and they were dreadfully over-crowded. I was able to write open letters to him and send through the German post and he was able to send prisoners' letters to England so I was really able to get more news of my family in England, through him. I could send him nothing of any use, as by then we were short of everything. Only onions were a delight to them, to flavour their terribly inadequate German stew. We were receiving Red Cross messages of course, but they were so limited and my only way of telling my family how thin I had got and how hungry I was, was confined to allusions to Mrs. Beeton. Many of these messages never reached us and often were censored, but my eldest daughter managed to let me know she had contacted one of those who came on the Commando Raid by saying she had news of Sophie Moffat's (my mother's maiden name) daughter from a recent visitor! We had now no paths open to the sea except at the harbour and we had to get a permit even to go there to collect sea water to cook with as our salt had run out. I cannot describe the taste of bread made with salt water. We were entirely without tea, coffee, soap and all clothes were getting worn out. It was a common sight to see the men wearing jackets made of old tablecloths and curtains and clothes were darned with wools of every conceivable colour. There were no shoes for the children so we just had to cut out the toes of their shoes as they grew, so as to allow the foot to poke out. Our shoes were re-soled with wood or with old tractor tyres.

In spite of all, the children were healthy. We had our beautiful milk from our Guernsey cows and I had many battles over full milk with the Commandant. As we had no fats, I protested every time they tried to seize more milk. Actually we had full milk until a month before the end. We had half a pint of full milk each a day when Guernsey only had skim four days a week. Our bread was reduced to three pounds each a week and meat two ounces a week. Our cows are always kept tethered so we had to spin the unwanted string usually used for tomato boxes into rope for the cows.

About this time, I had more trouble with the Germans about financing their electric light supply. They had made us take three engines from private houses and link them together to supply light for their troops. These engines were always breaking down and I finally wrote a very angry letter to the Commandant in Guernsey protesting about the cost to the Island. He did not come to face me himself about this but sent a very rough and uncouth officer from East Prussia who shouted at me that this was not the way to write to the Commandant. I put on a completely blank expression and said: 'If you shout I will not understand a word of what you are saying – and in England when we talk business, we never shout'. After that he was so surprised that he collapsed and we heard no more of these breakdowns of their supply. The lack of any light was the most terrible ordeal for people who just had to go to bed or sit by their firelight in gloom. The Sark people were never depressed and never for a moment doubted the ultimate victory of the Allies. The Germans commented on this to me. When the war began to go very badly for the Germans in Russia, they began to have grave doubts of their own victory. They ceased to sing as they marched along the roads. They gave me the impression of being secretly frightened as to what would be their position if they not only lost the war but were also held responsible for any bad treatment of us. Though outwardly they maintained all the forms and shams of invincibility.

Though I was now alone, do not imagine that I was afraid of the final victory of the Allies. I was still in possession of my house, my cattle and even my two dogs, who lived mostly on fish offal and potatoes. It was a long wait but I knew that the end was sure. We were very hungry at this time, but the Seneschal and I managed with the help of loyal helpers to get away with about a ton of wheat which we hid in my barn and ground on my farm mill in secret and issued secretly in the shops to people to supplement the inadequate bread ration. The worst was having no fuel for hot water. For baths we had to heat a cauldron in a backyard, fed with sticks and bits of gorse and for cooking we had only wood. The Germans were equally short of fuel and requisitioned a quantity of our trees, and they often chopped up and burned furniture which they looted out of the houses of people who had evacuated or been deported. We made up tobacco from clover heads, rose leaves, vine leaves or blackberry leaves which were also dried and used as tea, so were dried pea-pods. Coffee was made of fried barley with grated parsnip and sugar beet. Salt had to be collected from sea water and boiled down till it dehydrated – the drawback to this being that we had so little wood to use to boil it. At this time, we heard that wood was so scarce in Normandy that even coffins were only procurable with a permit issued by the local mayor.

The Germans began stealing our chickens, calves and pigs – even cats and dogs disappeared and were eaten by them but by this time, we had the knowledge that the landing in Normandy had taken place. My first information was actually brought to me by the German doctor. He appeared soon after my breakfast of fried mashed potato and closing the door of my study and looking very mysterious with a finger to his lips, he said that I must tell no one or he would be shot, but that the British and Americans had landed the other side of Cherbourg. He said it was probably only a raid like the one at Dieppe but he would come again and tell me. The moment he left we rushed to our radio set for the first time by daylight

From S. Hathaway, Sark Guernsey

Darling -

There is so much to do the weeks goes quickly.
I am hoping Olive + Lulu will come tomorrow.
Col. Knackfuss + Dr. Kratzer came to see me, +
I asked for them to be allowed to come, + the
former said yes, + he would phone Lulu when
he got back to Guernsey so they may just
turn up tomorrow. I hope for some Bridge, +
that our Curfew may be till 11. as it is too
early at 10. They asked for you + sent their
greetings! + brought me some cigarettes.
I am exchanging a pair of Ralph's grey flannel
trousers for cigarettes - 20 pkts, from Herbert
Baker who does not smoke! I hope you
have had your coat by now. If you need
more trousers tell Jehanne to get them for
you at Anderson + Sheppards. Tell her also
Steve is making a profit on the farm, over
+ above his wages + all expenses for seeds,
labour + fertilisers, (as I've just had a message
from Annie asking if he makes his wages).
I have been trying a jam experiment, with
Saccharine, no sugar, + Seaweed (strained)

Letter from Sibyl to Bob, 6th July 1943

and heard one of the hourly broadcasts. It was a terrific strain to say nothing about it but by this time, dozens of small crystal sets had been made up by directions given out by the BBC so that nearly every house had one hidden somewhere. Day by day we heard the guns and at night saw the flashes and lights. We watched the advance of these all along the coast of France opposite. It seemed to us a long time before Cherbourg fell.

Some of the German garrison, including the grim Admiral Hiefmayer, Hitler's personal friend, escaped from there at night and got to Guernsey to be a trial to us et it with - If it turns out O.K I will send you some. What do you get in that way in your parcels, & what sort of cigarettes? We have had no rain for a month, & need it badly, getting low in butter.

Jenny's cat mewed a lot the other night I think he will get rid of all the rabbits & rats soon The dogs will wear ribbons for your birthday and Buzz will be drunk on mine! Old Ibbotson gets madder than ever. He reads the Service in Church & last Sunday I hear he gave a Sermon on Diabetes! one of our lighter moments. I hope you & Wynne will see Markbreiter before me. Give Wynne my Love, & would you both like a box of onions we have some ready now. Nothing fresh from Lulu, Stewart doing a lot of work with the Gladys S's friends. Very profitably too.

All my very best love always. S.

Tell Wynne, he may not know, that the Cosbys have re-married each other, after ten ...

at the end. We used to watch the attacks on Cherbourg by the American planes, a lovely sight to us to see them coming in over our heads and swooping over Cherbourg and then to hear the thud and dull explosions which made our houses shake as Cherbourg is only some 22 miles as the crow flies. After the war, I asked some American officers who came to call on me, why it had taken so long, and was rather startled when he said it was partly the fault of one Julius Caesar who had built a rampart across the peninsula which the Germans had concreted and used as a sort of Maginot line.

AFTER D-DAY

After D-Day, we were completely cut off, no more food from France and almost no Red Cross messages. Appeals had been made by the Bailiffs of Jersey and Guernsey to the Red Cross but so far, nothing had happened and we were sure the Germans had not allowed these appeals to go through to our protecting power, Switzerland. The death rate in Guernsey began to be the highest ever and though, mercifully, there were no epidemics, medical supplies and anaesthetics ran out and people were eating minced potato peelings. There had been no soap for two years and the children were suffering from lice, scabies and impetigo. We had had no tea or coffee for three years and now money had no real value. A box of matches would fetch 10 shillings, the same price as a reel of sewing cotton. The Germans by now had used up most of their reserve stores, which were only sufficient for a three months' siege and began to requisition heavily from us.

Since the deportations our population was now only 363 and fortunately, the enemy needed milk as much as we did so they did not so far kill our cattle, but they requisitioned a big quantity of full milk, while we were supposed to have only half a pint per person a day. Needless to say that the farmers took care to skim the milk for the troops as much as they dared. When they complained that they could not make enough butter from the milk, I told them that I would go myself and see them churn it! They were horrified and when I arrived dressed in a white overall and armed with a large thermometer and gave them a lecture on buttermaking, they got so mixed up and confused that I never had another complaint.

The soldiers stole our vegetables and were really nearly starving, even eating cats. They broke into barns and houses and it was very alarming to me to see their discipline beginning to break down. We were really terribly hungry, often it was hard to sleep for the queer feeling of having a completely empty stomach. It was now time for the Red Cross to save us and it is quite impossible to describe our joy when the Swedish ship *Vega* chartered by the Red Cross at last arrived at New Year 1945. Nothing could ever taste so marvellous as our first 'Spam'. Sufficient parcels were brought in every fortnight for each person to have one. They contained a quarter pound sugar, half a pound butter, tea, raisins, prunes, corned beef or spam, chocolate, tinned milk, cheese, biscuits and salt but no flour. Immediately after we started to receive these parcels, the Germans cut down all our rations. They took 60% of our fish and gave us 40% and said they would take all our seed potatoes and 92% of others and cattle.

It became clear to us and them that the end of the war was near but the troops were to be seen feverishly dragging guns to new places. This state of things went on for five more months. Houses were demolished, wooden ones were burnt and anti-glider posts of iron girders and railway lines were put up in the fields, ruining our spring crops. These had small bombs on them and were called 'Rommel's Asparagus' by the troops.

It was astonishing to see how the spirits of the Germans varied from day to day. Sometimes one could hear them being ordered to sing which they did very unwillingly and then a few days later, when they had news of the V2s they altered completely. They were always being given pep talks by their officers. The admiral in command came over from Guernsey and addressed the troops vehemently, telling them they were to fight to the last and be the last Germans to surrender (which they actually were!) By 6th May the troops had become so disaffected that he only dared to address them in an open field after their arms had been piled aside. He told them that they would all be brutally treated if they were taken prisoners.

LIBERATION

It was now only a question of hours before the total surrender of Germany and it was very hard not to show openly our knowledge and our excitement. On May 7th we got our first order to deliver cattle next day and a requisition of 200 tons of timber trees to be cut for them and we never obeyed this order because we heard the next morning that Donitz had surrendered and by 11am I had the Union Jack and the Stars and Stripes flying from my tower. A gathering of all the inhabitants was quickly arranged by verbal messages and all assembled at the Island hall at 3pm to hear Mr. Churchill on the radio. We looked at each other and smiled when he said that the dear Channel Islands were free, because we still had 275 Germans all around us. Late that night we had a huge bonfire blazing on a most prominent spot on the cliffs, material for which had been quietly and secretly collected for some days beforehand. We heard afterwards from the navy that our bonfire which was the only one in the Channel Islands and actually the night before their surrender, had worried them a lot as they saw the glow from a distance north of Alderney and feared it was Germans carrying out sabotage.

German prisoners repairing La Coupee under the command of the Royal Engineers

In contrast, joy with British troops arriving at Creux harbour

The next day, we could see HMS *Beagle* lying at anchor off Guernsey harbour with other ships and a number of RAF planes circled over us dropping coloured flares, a great thrill for us, but the British troops did not actually land in Sark till May 10th, when owing to the Germans here refusing to answer any telephone calls from Guernsey, a rumour circulated there that there was 'trouble' in Sark, so at about 5pm that day a tug came over with three officers and 20 men and I went to the harbour to meet our Liberation force. Not a German was to be seen anywhere – the officer in charge asked where they were and for an interpreter. I was the only one and accompanied him to the house that the Germans used as their 'Kommandantur'. Not a German was around and not until one of our soldiers had knocked loudly, did they appear.

When they had, through me, answered all Colonel Allen's questions satisfactorily, he told me he could not leave any troops here as so far only a token force had been landed in Guernsey. He asked if I minded being left for a few days or would I go back to Guernsey with him. I replied that as I had been left for nearly five years, I could stand a few more days. He then told me to tell the German major who was in charge, that he was to carry out whatever orders I gave until our troops came over. I promptly ordered the telephone to be laid on to my house at once and kept open day and night so that I could contact Guernsey.

Next day, I gave orders to remove mines from the harbour and to give back our wireless sets and remove the anti-glider posts from among our crops. It gave me enormous satisfaction after all those years to be giving them orders on the

Dame Sibyl in 1963

telephone and saying 'repeat please' and then hearing them say 'Zur Befehl Gnadige Frau'. However, I was a little unsure, when after having ordered the removal of the roll-bombs hanging over the harbour and which the fishermen had told me were held by such rusty wire, that they might crash down when our troops were arriving. The Commandant telephoned to me to say that two of his soldiers had been killed doing this. I replied 'Just so?' and there was quite a pause and then he asked if they could be buried in our cemetery. I agreed to this but said that our gravediggers would make the graves, then another pause, and he asked if they could fire a volley over the graves. I was completely surprised and felt it was not an order that I had contemplated giving. So I had to telephone to Brigadier Snow who was in command of the Liberation forces and he gave his consent.

Next day, a launch was sent to take me to dine in HMS *Beagle* with Capt. Williams. I shall never forget that meal – no feast of Lucullus could ever have been like it and because when they had asked me what I missed most, I had said hot baths and the smell of frying bacon, I was given a special savoury of bacon, but it was nearly impossible to eat, one was so near tears and having had so little for so long, one just could not take it. I could not believe that the officers' collars and the tablecloth could be real as I had not seen anything that had been washed with soap for years.

So much work had to be done now in the Island and so many officials coming and going. The Ministry of Health were pleased at the condition of our children, but those who were getting their second teeth during the Occupation were unfortunate for our diet was so short of calcium.

I still had no news from my husband and I was beginning to get very anxious. I had learnt that Salzburg had been taken on the 3rd May so could not understand not hearing from him. Later, I found out they had been liberated by the American army and his letters had gone via the American Forces Mail (see later).

On 7th June, King George and Queen Elizabeth came to Guernsey. Everyone went crazy with delight, donned our pre-war garments and got out all the flags that we had kept hidden from the Germans. I had the privilege of being presented to the king and handing a Loyal Address from Sark and afterwards, having tea with him. He was very kind about my husband and promised to see that enquiries were made and his return should be speeded in every way. There was a large number of Russian prisoners in Guernsey. They had been used as slave labour and had been liberated and put into uniforms as they were almost in rags. They wished to be on the route where the king and queen would drive past and they cheered as lustily as any. The king told me that they were the first he had seen and he was struck by the different tone of their voices when cheering.

Five days after this, I had a telegram from my husband who had just been flown to London and he got back to Guernsey on 21st June. It was a wonderful re-union, but he looked terribly thin and nervy for some time, after his two and a half years in prison.

I want to say a little about what the Red Cross did for us and of how we helped ourselves over clothing. At the outbreak of war, we started a Red Cross workroom to which all my American friends subscribed most liberally. With these funds, we bought bales of flannel and wool in quantities. Up to the date of the Occupation, we had sent out 3,000 garments and pairs of socks and we still had a lot of material in hand which we hid in different helpers' houses. After a time when our needs became very urgent, we started a 'special aid' workroom and made up garments for the people who were in desperate need of clothing of all kinds. We also helped to fit out some of those who were being deported to Germany. We actually made 1,807 garments for men, women and children. Some of those deported were poor and needed help but all who could do so were ready to contribute to the cost of materials. Finally, these ran out and we could do nothing more for them.

Joy and gratitude which the people of Sark felt for their Red Cross parcels and help can be judged by the fact that they gave personally no less than £1,187 in collections – a very large sum when one considers there were only 363 people and no trade or tourists to help them exist. My generous American friends whose donations started our workroom, did a wonderful thing for us all.

Poem from a *Channel Island Review*, England

Sark
by Robert Dawson
November 1942

Sometimes when I'm in London, in my thoughts I'm far away,
Strolling down the little lane that leads to Dixcart Bay,
I travel there on wishes across the watery miles
That be between Southampton and the lovely Channel Isles.
The noises of the city beat harshly on the ear,
I'd rather hear the breaking of the waters green and clear,
The waves that fling their silver spray 'gainst rocks so grim and stark,
The surging of the restless sea around the Isle of Sark.
Someday I'll be returning to that beloved shore,
And from the little harbour, I shall climb the hill once more,
And see the fishing nets spread out to dry upon the grass,
And smell the honeysuckle in the hedges as I pass.

Frank and Hedy Collenette at St Sampson's Regatta in 1939

MEMORIES FROM SWITZERLAND

A big coincidence occurred way back in 1994 when Heidi Collenette and her sons, Brian and Samuel from Switzerland booked a holiday stay with my husband and I at our guesthouse Woodcote, Les Canichers. Heidi with two sons had a holiday in Guernsey the previous year and had bought my book A Child's War *she had no idea when she booked with us that I was the lady she had read about or my connection with the Occupation.*

The penny eventually dropped and with mutual interest, particularly with her sons, she told me in conversation that her father, Frank Collenette (a Guernseyman), had written his memoirs of the five years and would be happy to copy and send them to me. Although having kept them for quite a time, now is a good reason to go into print and Heidi has given me permission for her father's story to be printed. In the reading, it is obvious that he felt it was worthy of going into print, and it is in his own words as written.

Heidi's father, Frank, was born on 24th April 1915 and her mother, Hedy Lutz on 3rd July 1913 in Thal, Switzerland. She came to live and work in Guernsey in 1936 and married in 1938. Frank was born in a cottage at St. Andrews called Sunnymead. Heidi remembers her father saying that from the cottage there was a lovely view of the Atlantic. His memories are written of his time living at St Martins where he attended school and lived there from the age of 12.

Frank did not have a trade, money was short in the family and his work began at Frank Stroobant's shop in town (well known author of One Man's War*). He then went on to work as a bus driver in Alderney and after that, a driver for Creasey & Son in Guernsey and for a time, working at the airport for the Germans.*

The Sea Water Queue
An Occupation Story 1940–1945
by Frank Collenette

The sea was like a pond. The sun was starting on its way down to the west. We were sitting there on Vazon sea wall. All was so peaceful, not even a sound of the birds. We said to each other 'Will they come or won't they come?' We meant the Germans who now had France under their heel.

It was now getting towards the end of June. Almost all of the school children had been taken by ship to England. Their mothers were allowed to accompany them if they felt it their need. Of course, a lot stayed behind. For families who loved the way of life and not great riches, it was a hard path to take. Like driving a wedge into something that one knew would not part.

I worked then at a small vinery, as we say in Guernsey. We had four glasshouses – about 440 feet in all. I worked for a man who was known to be not so nice, however, to me he was just the opposite. He gave me full freedom at work. As my dad had been doing tomato work all his life, I soon picked it up.

Some boats were still coming to take what fruit they could to England. But they were always on the look-out for the Nazi planes or subs. People were still going away, but in the end, the States of Guernsey decided that some should stay. We got ready I believe, three times. But since then no boat to be seen. So we decided to stay, come what may. Some of our plants had to be cut down and the fruit thrown away. We thought the time would come when perhaps we could use the under glass for something else.

In my writing, I do not want to follow along with exact dates. I want more to write about what the poor really had to live on. Because if one had had a shop or store with at least tobacco and cigarettes by the cwt, then one wondered if they lived another kind of life.

The Irish fusiliers had gone, so sitting on this wall at Vazon Bay we knew we were lost to the Germans if he came or not. There would not be a lot to be got out of Guernsey but Hitler could tell his people 'We are in England' even if he was not. This is just what he did, using such places as Midland Bank and London Shipping Office as his background to make-believe. Men sitting alongside of me were smoking their loved pipes or cigarettes, we wondered for how long. It was just that one sentence, wait and see. As almost half the Islands' population had left, our stocks would last longer if no one got their hands to them. The I.F. Evening meal was calling us so we all wished each other 'Cheerio, sleep well' and we each went our own ways.

I needed to go to St Peter Port about four miles away, to get to, Hedy (my wife) and home. Before we were married, we had lived at Le Vallon Road at Number 10. We had spent many happy hours there with very nice neighbours. They had a son called Ronnie. This family stayed together and during the Occupation, lived at Saints Road. With all the sadness and shortages which the Occupation brought, we spent many lovely and amazing evenings with this family. Well, on the evening of June 27th 1940, Hedy my wife and I went down to see the cattle (well any kind of animal) that could be saved from the Island of Alderney, which were being unloaded from boats that were big enough for this. We had no idea that the next evening would be the most tragic evening for Guernsey. From our little house in the Rue du Pre, we had heard the soldiers (that were billeted here) when they had left to go back to England. We did not know then, how near we were to other marching feet.

No more waiting now. During the late afternoon and evening of June 28th, the Germans bombed St Peter Port harbour. On the harbour were many lorries full of tomatoes. Drivers went under for safety and got burnt alive. Over 30 people lost their lives. Their bombing was very poor – they were well away from real targets.

It was Hedy who saw the bombs at first. Outside of our cottage door she said 'Look something is coming out of those planes!' Many days before we had seen planes with those awful crosses on them, flying sometimes quite low. But we never imagined this! We were really afraid of the Germans because we had heard how they had treated other occupied countries.

During the evening, English planes flew low over the Island. We also heard that Mr Churchill had said over the radio that the Channel Islands were free Islands and in no way fortified. However, the mail boat had been in harbour. It had one anti-aircraft gun aboard. The Germans knew that they were being fired at.

We were now at my mother's place at Le Vallon, Number 10. On the Saturday, June 29th 1940, Hedy went to do some shopping. When she arrived back home, my father told her 'If you go out again when German planes are about, I will be really cross with you!' Hedy just smiled and said 'They are not after me.'

Cows had been put to graze on the airport. This was an idea that the Germans would not think there was an airport there. The RAF had been there and on leaving blocked waterways, as the airport was without concrete runways, the airport would flood in the winter months. The next day was Sunday, June 30th and all seemed so quiet. My father said to me 'Will we go out with our bikes for a ride somewhere?' We had only ridden about 1 mile away from home when we saw German soldiers with bikes. They had a pile of leaflets under their arms which they issued to passers-by. It stated that the German army, navy and air force had taken Guernsey in occupation. So long as we respected them, they would respect us. It was once again, wait and see.

I wrote a few sentences ago that animals had been taken off Alderney. The reason for this was that all except for two or three Alderney people, they had all left and gone to England, the Island being so near to France it was the safest way.

People left in panic, houses were left open. It was just pack and go. My Mother who had heart trouble did not feel so well. She had to have a medicine which she

German band playing at Munro's on the Esplanade, St Peter Port

thought she would not get under the Germans as it would be off-ration and not be able to be had for the civil population. My sister had left Guernsey and was now in England. Her husband was in the army. He had advised her to get away from Guernsey. My father put the big drum of St Martins Band under his bed as he thought it would be safe there. My sister had won two lovely silver cups. She was Guernsey's running champion. They were hidden as well.

It is a new chapter indeed. We were going to see if the Germans had respect for us or not. It would be a job for us to have a real respect for them. They were now on the Island and at the airport. They had been to our Bailiff.

My tomato work came to an end and we were told that the States of Guernsey would find jobs for the men at least. We had heard that our best Doctor was on his way up the gangway before the Germans came. But he was asked to stay and he did – we must be very thankful that he did. He did a wonderful job under such conditions. We found out through the newspaper now taken over by the Germans that we could keep our radios until further notice. As usual, if we were not good, we would have them taken away. We were told that if people could live together more than at present, that would save gas and electric. So we were with mum and dad for a few months.

But in such a small flat, it was a bit too much for the four of us. So we took an empty place nearby in the State's houses. I was soon to learn that I could go and help on farms. I was not used to this kind of work but soon got used to it. Also the name of each cow. It surprised me how I could get to know the difference when quite a few cows were in the fields! The first farm I worked at was near Icart. I had nice workmates here but could not stay after a few months and had to change.

These first few days of Occupation worried us, this word RESPECT. Every day, big carrier planes arrived, taking away what they could lay their hands on. But the worst was the food. So that we got to learn that instead of two years' stores in hand, it had dwindled down to six months. We then knew that our glasshouses would have to be turned into vegetable gardens if we were to survive. It was good that all of us had read or heard about *Robinson Crusoe* because now we were in the same state as he was. In this house where we lived, the garden was quite big but because we had no real ground manure, the crops did not do well, the potatoes were small. However, lots of people took over gardens from people who had gone off. The Germans did not live in buildings that the RAF would attack such as Fort George, the Castle etc, they forced people who had room to take them in. Friends of ours were made to give up their own double bedroom to two soldiers. The officer who came to look at the room told the wife the room had to stay as it was. She asked 'Can't I take away my eiderdown – it is a wedding present?' He said no and of course, she cried.

However, when the two soldiers arrived, they let her have different things she wanted to have. But it was never the same with those two there. She was also expected to do their dirty washing – of course she was paid at least.

I also delivered meat for Chilcott, the butcher at their St Martins shop till we had no more petrol for motorbikes and also almost no meat. One lady told me that she had quite a nice officer in her house. But he would walk in with nailed boots over her best carpet and played her piano. To tell him was useless. My sister Ruth had a spaniel which of course she had to leave behind – he was called Laddie. He was having a job to live with no dog food to be had. If there was any food about of any kind, then the Germans had to know or one got into trouble. They believed they were here to defend us, so our Island had to feed them.

Quite early in the Occupation, they had marched through the town with their band. What we had heard of the band, it was good. The band master we noticed never gave the Hitler salute when playing. As far as I knew, he married a Guernsey girl and went to England after the war. The show must go on under all trouble.

Concerts were organised at Candie Gardens and also at the Lyric Cinema by local singers etc. We spent many happy and unforgettable evenings there. We thank them all. Each programme had to be censored by the Germans. We had many laughs over this. There was a little orchestra at the Lyric which used to play tunes picked up from England even when the time came that the radios were forbidden. The Gaumont Cinema and the Regal were taken over by the Germans. After about six weeks of occupation, the British attacked the airport. We were told if true, that this was to show the Germans that England still had a hand on the Channel Islands. We heard that a few had been killed up there. The real number will never be known.

Hedy more than me was noticing the strict food rations. The bread was not enough and the milk was getting weak as the cream was getting taken off for butter. Some girls who went with the Germans said that a German was eating butter out of the paper packing like chocolate. I once saw one eating grapes – he was holding the whole bunch over his open mouth. We could not get grapes for love or money. It made one's heart ache. We would have also wished we had had a baby because Hedy would have had good milk, butter etc. People like me could apply for hard workers' rations but it was hardly worth the trouble, perhaps just a few ounces of cheese or meat a week. Very often when a farmer went into his stable in the morning early to milk his cows, they were dry or foodstuffs and vegetables would be taken. Early one morning when still dark, I turned on the stable lights, there were two Germans there. They said 'Gut Morgan' quite politely and disappeared at once. When the cows were milked, we found out why they and perhaps others had been there milking the cows.

Xmas Party
The Lyric's Seasonable Show for the Island

PART I.

Christmas Overture on a Melody of Gounod and Xmas Carols
for Orchestra and Voices arranged by F. COLLET.

a) Les anges dans nos campagnes.
b) The First Nowell.
c) Adeste Fidelis.

Soprano	Miss Gertie Duquemin
Alto	Miss Daphne Brache
Tenor	Mr. Rex Priaulx

Peter Campbell presents

"Old Year Out"
A Fantasy by
MOLLIE RENOUF.

CAST :

The Child	Isobel Cecilia
The Mother	Mollie Renouf
The Old Man	Wilfred Shirvell
Spring	Daphne Collivet

(Pupil of Miss Joyce Ferguson)

Summer	Gwen Smith
Autumn	Maureen de Caudeville
Winter	Jessie Marriette

Produced by Mollie Renouf.
Music arranged by Fred Collet.

Incidental Music to the Fantasy Play—REVERIE by Claude Debussy

Spring—Pizzicati from the Ballet "Sylvia" *Delibes*
Summer—Summer Days Suite, 3rd movement *E. Coates*
Autumn—3, 4 Waltz-Suite, No. 6 *Coleridge-Taylor*
Winter—Ballet Music from "Faust" *Gounod*

Spring : Miss Daphne Collivet. Summer : Miss Gwen Smith
Autumn : Maureen de Caudeville. Winter : Miss Jessie Marriette

PART II.

THE PARTY :

Our Jovial Lord	Peter Campbell
Leeves, the Butler	Ted Boielle

The Guests :—Lilian Brache, Douglas Luckie, Jessie Marriette,
Pearl and Gwen Smith, The Brache Sisters, Will. Shirvell and—
Sebastian –home from the sea– Cyd Gardner.

Also Invited—

Freddie Chesters—home from L— — who will sing two songs written
and composed by Ernie Webster (late Saxophonist and Clarinet
player of the Lyric Theatre Orchestra,) and Isobel Cecilia (pupil of
Miss Dorothy C. Hurrell).

FUN AND GAMES FOR ALL
—— and ——
CYD AND PETE CRACK THE CRACKER.

PERSONNEL OF ORCHESTRA :

Leader Violin	Miss Laura Hillman
Ripiano Violin	Mr. Len Gould
'Cello	Mr. J. Hillman
Clarinet	Mr. Roland Timms
Alto Saxophone	Mr. Austin Mann
Tenor Saxophone	Mr. W. Shepperd
Trumpet	Mr. George Mabire
Bass and Tuba	Mr. A. Reeve
Drum and Effects	Mr. H. Tuckwell
Tubular Bells	Mr. W. Shepperd
Piano	Mr. Clifford Ferbrache

Conductor : FRED COLLET (Solo Violin.)
Music Score of XMAS PARTY ... Fred Collet.

Now we were not so fussy with the food so that animal carrots etc always helped a lot. I remember well on one farm where I worked, at the Villette, there had been sides of cattle, twenty-two pigs and some hens. I was told one day that if I helped to kill a pig, I would get 2lb of pork to take home. I could never kill, also it was my job to clean out those pigs, big and small, each day and also to feed them. I said I could not help even if I lost my job. I did not lose my job but my meat. However, you can just imagine having one egg in your trouser pocket for about three hours and work with it there, so I could take it home just to have the joy of it. Hedy and I having an egg to eat again. We also believed one egg would do our health wonders.

Hedy being Swiss we found out that many Swiss were still on the Island, we got in touch with them and visited them on different evenings during the week. We spent many happy hours this way. Of course we had our Guernsey friends as well and relations. But some of our most friendly relations had gone to England. So our fun with them at the beach near the castle had gone until peace came again. Well the Germans took away food, they brought back cement from France. We could not eat that! The cement factories in France must have been working overtime to make the stuff.

Some people were still getting away to England by fishing boat or other types of boat which they believed could take them there. They, the fishermen, had a petrol ration although small some managed to put a little aside for this escape. So in fog or deep in the really black nights, some went off to England. This did not help us because the Germans put up orders as big as posters everywhere that they would take all the young men away if this happened again. However, these people helped England because they brought news of the goings on in Guernsey, Alderney and Sark. There were a few Germans in Sark but they said the Dame could speak German like a German so she told them where they stood in their own tone of speech. To take away a lot of young men to the continent would have only hurt themselves as well as a lot of Guernseymen as some were forced to work for them. I must say a lot of young men had been to England to join up before the Germans came, but they were sent back for a while because England had not enough uniforms, rifles, etc at that time. I myself had been exempt from the Guernsey soldiers. The Guernsey Militia was disbanded. The Jersey Militia was taken on by the Hampshire Regiment.

Up to now, I have forgotten to say that we had a curfew. We had to be in at 10pm and stay inside the house until 6am in the morning. On no account were we even to go into our own garden or we may be shot. During winter time, we were very often in the road or through lanes that I knew well after these hours. However, not longer than perhaps fifteen minutes. It was always hard to break up after a lovely evening. At these times, we always felt we belonged more to each other. We were all in the same boat now. Of course, people with farms, gardens or glasshouses or even shops could exchange goods between each other, they were a bit better off. Soon the Germans started bringing over from France, foreign labour. Some of these poor looking men without proper clothes or footwear had come from all over occupied Europe to work on German bunkers etc. We did not know how long we would still be able to have our radios. Lord Haw Haw from Germany was a laugh. He was British and tried to put over a lot of lies being well paid by the Germans. The stuff he tried to tell us. By what he said, England did not exist anymore.

Rabbits were being kept by many people as well but we would exchange them for other food, we could not eat something like a pet. We also had a cat, a lovely black and white Persian. She was ever so good. She can't have been so happy with cooked cabbage leaves but she gave us the idea she did like them, when we had no meat juice or fish pieces. We were rationed for clothing, but the Germans bought a lot of our clothes. It was said in a shop that the Germans had said that he was having a suit made in London. The shops soon got empty this way. Their wives and sweethearts in Germany soon had to give up the idea of having nylon stockings from Guernsey. The States formed a committee that now should go to France and take up trade agreements with the French. Well, we could offer them no goods just money which if not enough would be a debit to be paid back after the war. The German money was what we called Hitler money. He printed what was known as Occupation Marks. They were of no value. All money we put into post or banks was written down in Guernsey cash or British then. This debt was on Guernsey's shoulder till after the war when we would have to settle up. Guernsey also printed its own money.

Times started to get a bit harder. My father still had his work in the glasshouses. They planted cabbage, lettuce etc. In season it was lovely to see all these vegetables but we must say the outdoor ones were of a better taste. Dad brought home worry and kept us thinking 'I wonder' and we wondered what would happen too. We planted in hope to keep us alive and the Germans always came and claimed a big share. If there were three houses full of carrots then they took one house and often took more. Of course, this and other happenings like this were kept in the family not to worry other people. We knew that the Germans had to eat but they had no need to be here. For what reason? They brought three big guns that could fire about twenty-five to thirty miles I believe. They could not reach England's coast with them. Our RAF plans knew they were there and no ship with any sense would go so close as to be hit by one of these guns. I saw these guns, or one of them, going up Carmel, St Martins, with German sailors sitting like on horseback on the barrel. I was not afraid they would destroy English ships. I was more worried about how much vibration these things make and cause damage to houses and glasshouses. They never knew that they were being photographed but we still know what they looked like as there is none to be seen now after the war.

However some food did start to come from France but sad to say, the French thought that some food was for the Germans so tins were holed and other food damaged. So it all had to be put to the test before it came to us. The cheese was usually sweet of a strong taste so that a lot of people did not want it. Hedy and I liked it well enough. Well, when we have not a lot to eat, we eat almost anything. I ate a lot of salad during the war, I had not liked it before. I thought I would always like it but I gave it up as soon as other food was about. We could eat as many tomatoes as we liked, many free of charge but they were not filling. Some was given to the cows so that when they ate so many, the milk was a little pink instead of white.

As the German uniform was a dark green, they usually had grey flannels on which we are sure must have come from our stocks so that it came that we could buy no more grey flannel in our shops. Shoes became a problem. Some came from France, a lot with wooden soles though. We were too proud even then to wear wooden shoes on a Sunday. So, like others did as well, we removed the wooden soles from the upper and when possible, put leather from an old machine belt in its place. Hedy still had a pair on Liberation. We also put soles on shoes or boots made from bike tyres. When we had no bike tyres, we made some from water hoses. A bit heavy but on the front tyre it was not too bad with a real tyre on the back. This valve rubber was the insulating rubber of electric wire. If this wire happened to have a woven case over the rubber when removed, we used these as boot or shoe laces. It got hard to mend a puncture as it was getting almost impossible to get the rubber glue. This was made by a few Guernseymen by melting yellow rubber from shoe soles. It was not as good as the real one but it was better than nothing. There was also the Guernsey tyre which was made from thick motor tyres sewn on to cycle tyre wires. They were very clear though.

Our radios had to be given up. We did not have one but mum and dad did. This was really a new chapter in our lives. However, all were not given in. The news still leaked out somewhere. Some radio shops were still kept open as they offered their services to the Germans. This was not to be friendly. When a German brought his radio to be repaired if he could not get a sound out of it, the Guernsey man said he had done all he could but it was beyond repair. The German radios in almost all cases were our sets. Our radio man took good pieces out for his hidden radio then put broken parts in the Germans. In this way Guernsey was kept up with English news. We are sure that some Germans did not believe all Goebbels spat out. Possibly they listened to our side sometimes. Most of the shops in Guernsey kept open. They decorated their windows with adverts to fill up the space as they were afraid the Germans would take over their shop. A lot of shops turned themselves into exchange shops but one had to have food or cigarettes or tobacco to get a good exchange. We had heard that our First German Commandant had a Scottish wife. We don't know but when he went they said he was too good to us so perhaps it was true about the wife. The Germans brought over French girls and three houses were used by them – one at George Road, one near Icart and one along the front sea road, towards Richmond. No civis were allowed there – only soldiers. Perhaps for the decent Guernsey or English girl, this was good in its way because many men had been worried about their women being attacked by Germans. We had heard about this in other occupied countries but we don't think it happened in Guernsey. We also heard that in other countries, the Germans had stolen fur from women on the roads or forced them in their homes to give up fur but in Guernsey it did not happen. Hedy had a short one because she always felt so cold. It was said amongst people that the Germans had been warned that they were going to live with British and to behave themselves. How true this was, we did not know but there seemed to be all the reason to believe it.

We had left our State's house and now lived in a cottage near Luff's grocery store. As I have said, our neighbour friends had a son called Ronnie. He liked making models out of Meccano. I had quite a lot and very often he came to us there and spent the evening with us. Because of the curfew he stayed sometimes overnight. We were glad that his parents let him come as we had no child of our own. I was also interested in slides and films, even trying to make our own projector. Then we were to hear that a lot of people in Guernsey had Pathe films and machines. I was really interested. We also heard that about 200 films could be got hold of and put into a library and to be let out at 1/- per reel of film. I had no Pathe projector but in Grut's Photo Shop there was an incomplete one in the window. I looked at it and at once saw that I could fix the rest up with Meccano. With a bit of a tight fit with money, Hedy went and got me that projector. Well, what I got done with Meccano proved itself, it worked almost perfectly. The take up of film was the trickiest job not to get it to jerk or pull to break film. However, with rubber rings each side of films spool, it was just the thing. So we went to the library in the arcade and got two or three films. We chose comedians such as Charlie Chaplin, Laurel and Hardy as a start. This gave us light in the darkness; now we could have some laughs! I decided it would be nice to show some of the films to people we knew as well and of course our friends. So we did this going up to Ronnie's family amongst them. We went also to a cripple lady who could not walk. Of course there were films that they did not like sometimes. It gave me pleasure though to show these many times, and they wanted to help pay for films. We had one very lovely film that I remember about that was an airship trip over the Atlantic, filmed from the ship.

Trouble for 'Fritz'

The Germans had also issued a notice that all Swiss or Swiss-born persons could return to Switzerland on a certain date. This would only take place once all Swiss who wanted to go should report to the Commandant's office. Hedy and I talked it over. She was now British through marriage but born Swiss. In the end, she said she would not go. We didn't know how long this war would go on. We wouldn't know where we could meet after. So those that wanted to go left but quite a lot stayed behind and some of these we still visited in the evenings. One Swiss had been chief waiter at the Royal Hotel. He had married a Guernsey person. They had four nice children and all were with them here in Guernsey. Fritz worked for the Germans but not because he liked it. It was because he knew their language, perhaps they had forced him, we don't know. However, there was quite a good lot of trouble between him and the Germans. Fritz had kept chickens to help feed his four children, also it was nice to have an egg sometimes. But because of no proper food, the hens did not always lay. One night, Fritz heard a noise. He went outside and two Germans were after his chickens. He attacked them at once. He was a well-built man – it was no fun to have trouble with Fritz. Still, the Germans got away in the end. But I am not sure if both lost their caps, or just one of them. However, Fritz telephoned the Commandant at once and gave him the name and number inside the cap. Or if there was no name, he gave him the number. The Commandant knew at once who this was. He said 'Fritz (on the telephone) – this man or men will be sent to the Russian front at once!' This was not the only time that Fritz came into contact with the Germans. Fritz also kept rabbits in a yard. Around the yard was quite a high wall and along the top of the wall broken glass had been pressed into cement to stop anyone getting over the wall. However when Fritz woke up in the morning once, going outside he found out that someone had taken his biggest rabbits, even mother rabbits that had quite small ones. He was once again quite sure it was the Jerries. He told some of his nearest men friends about an idea but he did not ask me because I had my wife there with me. The Germans kept rabbits as well not so far away in a farm they had taken over in the Hubits. They decided they would steal as many rabbits from the Germans as they could. They got organized! Fritz was to talk to the guard in the road while his four pals did their job in the farmyard. Fritz kept the guard talking well till the job was done. Each man that went had a sack with the rabbits to take home. However, something went wrong they had not thought about. The German guard must have gone to the rabbit boxes after and notified the Commandant. Because on the way home some men were stopped by the Germans and asked what they had in their sacks and of course, they had to show the Germans the contents. The Guernsey chaps tried to keep Fritz out of it all, but the guard and Commandant would not believe them. They were ordered to go to prison for a long time. Fritz had been pulled about in the German office, and almost spat at, but he was let off because of his four children. The Guernsey chaps could not go to jail at once because the jail was over full and had to wait their turn. The Jerries punished people for almost nothing. Fritz possibly made them wild because he always held with the British. He had a right to believe in something nearer the truth as to what the Germans printed on the front of our newspaper.

Fritz's children very often left their toys etc out in the garden. They had some real leather reins for the smallest child. These were left and forgotten. Next morning they were gone. We know that the Germans were after anything of value – gold, silver etc because they could get it with this paper money that was of no use. It did not cost Germany anything, the debt went on Guernsey. However, he was sure that the Germans had turned on their hate again. Fritz turned on his again. Fritz's wife told Hedy and me that Fritz knew where the Germans had a store of oil and petrol in a big hole in a field. It was covered with branches of trees to camouflage them. Fritz went one dark night and rolled a 100 gallon barrel of petrol home without being caught. We noticed that he rode his AJS motorcycle for a very long time when others could not! However, if stopped, he said he worked for the Germans. Fritz was very strong willed. He kept a tin of Club cigarettes on his mantelpiece for Liberation Day. He would not open it till then, he said. He also filled a water hose with cement and said the next German who steals from little children will get this on his head. Fritz's wife was worried because she told us he would kill a German that way. However, glad to say he never used it. It was always handy though on a shelf in the sitting room!

MAKE DO AND MEND!

It was while we lived in this cottage near Luff's Stores in St Martins that I had the idea of finding out how a shoe was made so I took one apart. With some waste leather and oilcloth and of course a few nails, I made a little sandal and shoe with felt top. Hedy and I thought they were quite good to say, but I thought if I am to make more, I must at least be able to get some little nails from somewhere. Like almost everything in this occupation, we had to hunt for it, sometimes like a pin in a haystack. In the end, a shoe shop would sell me some and I used to buy one pound at once but this was also a mistake. They said after a while I could not have any more. However, before this had happened I had made 120 pairs of little shoes and sandals for children. I must say that some were not all that good and there was a lot of talk about what I made. Some women gave me nice leather bags to cut up to make shoes and, by what they told me afterwords, the shoes were no good. However, it was the *Star Newspaper* who told me I should go to the welfare office with the first I made. This I had done and they put orders with me at once, both for sandals and shoes and still wanted more when nails ran out. However, there was one thing in my favour and that was the price. I was asking only half the price of those they managed to get over in France. The French ones were said to be no good at all as far as the uppers were concerned. I had enjoyed the work and would have tried to do more if only the nails had not run out. I also made a few wooden toys with wood that I had about. Hedy had bought me a fret saw with luck at Leale's in the Bordage, but it soon got that we could not buy anymore saw blades.

At this time, we had noticed that the ration of fish would be given out at other places than the fish market. We don't know if this was to keep the Germans away from our supplies. I had to go to St Andrews once for fish, quite near the church and if I had not had a bike, I would have had quite a long walk. The food kept on getting less all the time. We could not do anything as far as food was concerned without the Germans having their noses in it. We were told that if we made long trenches in the ground and filled them with potatoes, they would store for quite a while, so we did this. One day when I was passing the field where this was being done, I saw something that would make anyone's blood boil, as we say. We were putting potatoes at one end of the trench and covering them up and the Germans were taking them out at the other end and filling their lorries, without a thought of how we would live. The Germans must have known we were short because some women, sorry to say, went with the Germans. But we believe in very many cases, it was for food or to beg for food. We were not supposed to have a few little stocks of anything in the way of food. We had friends who buried a box full of tinned food in their little greenhouse in front of the front door. The German officers who went on search were standing talking to our friend near the front – about two feet under his feet was this food. Peter, her husband, blocked up a space in the kitchen, for what this space was there for we don't know. However, Peter printed these boards the same colour as the rest of the kitchen. What was behind these we're not sure of but at least a few hundred cwts of pots were stored there! Peter said he was not planting potatoes to feed the Germans. Whenever we visited them we had a nice meal.

Hedy used to get me a book for Christmas or for my birthday. One that she got me was called *Thunder Ahead* written by that famous racing driver called Malcolm Campbell. It was a really interesting book. There were a lot of chapters about the race track, Brooklands, near Weybridge in Surrey, England. I had always followed a lot of the goings on at Brooklands. Second-hand books were easy to get, even some grocery shops used to sell some. In some shops, they used to buy them so as to always have some to sell. One shop in Mansell Street at the top of Mill Street was a shop like this. I got some lovely books there and when I did not want them I took them back. The shop also sold anything that might be of use to anyone else in times like these. We always could have something to read,

MILITÄR - KONZERT

„ Froher Klang zum Sonntagabend "

AM SONNTAG, DEM 11. JULI 1943,

abends 20.00 Uhr in

CANDIE GARDENS

Es spielt das Musikkorps eines Grenadier-Regimentes unter der Leitung von Obermusikmeister Gerhard Anders.

MILITARY CONCERT

" Merry Notes for Sunday Evening "

CANDIE GARDENS

SUNDAY, JULY 11th, 1943,

at 8 p.m.

Music by a Regimental Band, under the conductorship of Bandmaster Gerhard Anders.

" Press " Pa. 405.

Military concerts were given and were enjoyed by both Islanders and Germans

German band playing outside the French Halles, market

true stories if we wanted them, instead of all the fairy-tales the Germans put on our daily newspaper. We had to have the newspaper because we would have lost the idea of how many times it was forbidden to do this or that. Every day there must have been some thing VERBOTEN on it.

While I helped the farmers as well, there was a big field near Fort George on the Fort Road. It was a lovely big field, always a lot of crops there. Many people talked about this field, how well kept it was. Well, we put in some potatoes there. A day or two after this, the Germans were at their game again. They put two or three (I am not sure now) anti-aircraft gun posts right in the middle of the potato field. They used a machine to scoop out the ground so that potatoes flew in all directions.

We would think someone was gone raving mad doing this but they would possibly have said this is for defence. Workmen had said amongst each other that in a field in St Andrew's they had put up a few anti-aircraft guns. These 'guns' were only telephone and telegram poles made of wood. They said that the RAF had dropped wooden bombs in this field. However, the RAF planes did some good work at photographing. They once dropped plans as leaflets at the airport showing the underground petrol tanks with a cross. The RAF must have seen them at work on these.

Windmills were being put up to make light. Not very big ones of course with a belt leading on to a pulley fixed on a cycle dynamo. Sometimes some tried to charge a car battery with wind, but it took a lot. There was also football being played with a few local teams. One or two games were played against the Germans but we soon put them off. The local chaps did not have the food, we did not feel it was right playing against people like this. Starve one, then invite them to play football! Different halls in the Island tried to put on plays or shows to keep the people happy. One play called *The Ghost Train* at the Little Theatre was ever so good. It was really good what was put over on the stages sometimes during the Occupation. A lot of attics must have been turned and turned over to find material in all that appeared during these plays. Even a musical written by a local man was ever so good, *Meikereids, Lone Across the Atlantic* I think it was called. The scenery could have been pre-war.

Now in Guernsey the people had been left with no coffee or tea so parsnips, carrots and blackberry leaves were tried. They were dried and then put into water like one makes tea. Of course I must say the parsnips and carrots were grated. Tobacco got scarce as well. It could only be bought through exchange of food or on the Black Market. German cigarettes were seen in the windows of the Black Market shops because the Germans sometimes gave them to get something he could not get himself.

PERMITS TO ENTER!

My brother had been working at the airport for quite a while. He would not say what he was doing up there but there must have been something big going on because hundreds of planes landed there and went off again.

However, what I had always feared happened one day. I was told I had to go to work at the airport. My brother told me to keep with him whenever possible. We had to parade each morning, about 300 of us, then be sent off to different jobs. We were guarded by an armed German soldier. I soon found out what was going on so I could soon answer my mother's questions in a free and true way, also my wife's. My wife believed she knew what could be going and I saw that they were building fighter plane hangars as we had to help with this. They were being made with a wooden frame with tarpaulin stretched over. There was enough wood to be had at the saw mills about Guernsey. The Germans did not have to ask. They just took whatever they needed. We had to get ready the bottom of the hangars where blocks of Guernsey granite were being put because the RAF had left the airport with blocked drains so that the planes would have been in much water at different times of the year. The permit that the Germans issued for us to enter the airport showed no signs of 'You must come'. It just said that Mr Collenette was working at the airport and was allowed to pass the guard. Doing parade in the mornings, the Germans noticed that my brother and I wanted to keep together, sometimes they even laughed to see us edging together. It very often happened that we did work together.

It happened once that we got a very nice guard with us who cleaned up a corner of the airport. At 9 o'clock the German took out his sandwich and started to eat. He told us to stop for a while to eat as well. Through my wife I could speak a little German, Swiss German is not quite the same, but I could get him to understand that we had not enough to eat and could not bring a sandwich with us.

During this spell a big plane (we called them carrier planes) used as soldier, officer, transport carriers, etc, also for cargo of which more was taken out as was brought in landed. I made this soldier understand and said 'Why don't you get into that plane and go home?' He said he had a wife and two children and had not seen them for so long. We actually saw tears in his eyes. I told him war was a dirty affair and no good to anyone. He agreed.

Very often we got the Germans laughing, if only doing things with our hands. We noticed that they treated us a lot better than those poor foreign workers they brought over. One day it had rained very hard, like thunder rain. We were most of us wet through. I had a good pair of clogs with leather tops but the soles got so soaked that my feet were really wet. Some workmen came to me and asked me if, as I could talk a little German, I could ask the German officer if we could go home today. So I said I would, so when he came along I put it over to him as nice as I could. I said 'Sir, these men are all wet and will get ill if they carry on today in this weather.' He stood at least and listened to what I had to say. Then he walked off without giving me an answer. I thought, like my workmates, we had had it. However, before he got to the airport buildings, he blew on his whistle and shouted, 'All go home'. Well, we could have kissed him. He possibly was not a hard-boiled Nazi like we believed most of them were.

I have very often thought since that this 'knowing a bit of German' could get me into trouble because I could understand most of what the Germans said to each other. They also asked me why I knew German. I told them my Swiss wife taught me some in the Swiss dialect. I could have asked them for what reason they spoke such good English but we all knew why. Hitler had needed this and would need them to speak English since he was going to take over the whole world.

When our soldiers had pulled out of France at Dunkirk (because of the Germans), Mr Churchill and the soldiers said 'we will be back' and this we all believed. But the Germans had had to give up the idea of the England invasion now that the Russian Front was too much to tackle at once. Hitler did not help himself at all by getting rid of all the Jews in concentration camps. The Jews came from all countries and this made the hate against him a lot worse. Americans also knew that if Hitler ever got there, he would be after a large part of their nationality, being Jews. The Battle of Britain had also been a mistake by the German Goering with his air force. (They still had some planes, but had lost so many over England in this battle that it was not actually planes now it was pilots and petrol). Also, the Germans believed the Tommy would return, that is why the Atlantic Wall was built. The Germans also had a wall, the Ziegfried Line but nothing like this Atlantic Wall. Even the British were singing now: 'We are going to hang out our washing on the Zeigfried Line if the Ziegfried Line is still there.'

Once we counted hundreds of planes flying in formation towards England. The air seemed to vibrate, we had nice words for them, whereas Germans cheered! We could not understand how the Germans, who are a well educated race of people, could believe all the news they were supposed to believe. I knew that lorries had to go to St Sampson's stone, crushing machines to get stone for the floors of these new hangars. So I thought I will get away from this place before anything happens. We knew that our RAF boys would do all they could to bomb when Guernseymen were not at the airport. There were always planes about. Every so often, and on different German installations, we were being attacked by our own planes. They worried the Germans off and on, however, what could be a drawback were the times the Germans used to make us take dinner from 12 to 1. Usually we had dinner in Guernsey a bit later. However I managed to get on a lorry, so except for unloading I was away from the place. We were one driver and two or three men to load. The rides, I must say, I enjoyed very well except when the weather was bad. Some of us had to be on the stones in the back. However one day just after 1pm we heard planes, but could not see them because of cloud. Then all at once we did not hear the motors anymore but we did hear the next noise, through the bombs of course! They were after these new hangars and no wonder as the sail cloth tarpaulin had been painted just like a glasshouse. But of course the RAF knew that no Guernsey glasshouse was built that shape.

Besides Germans, a few Guernsey men were killed. I was quite near the Airport Hotel leaning against the lorry when it happened. I ran towards the hotel. The kitchen door of the hotel had a cement shelter roof. A German girl told me to come under the cement roof and as soon as it was all over, I went for my bike and went home. The RAF must have thought we were away at dinner.

Next morning when we went to work we were told to go home again for the morning and come again in the afternoon. We saw then that the wooden barracks up there had been holed with machine gun fire and the Germans had nailed tin covers over these holes during the morning. How many Germans died we never knew. After this I did not feel well. I had stomach trouble and had to go to our family doctor. I say 'family doctor' because he had been all my life up to now, the only doctor I knew. At once he asked me if I had been working at the airport. He said 'Ah, that's it', he believed it was the cause. He asked me if I would like to come away from the airport but I answered 'How can I do this doctor? The Commandant is the boss in Guernsey now?' He said, 'Frank Collenette, if I give you a letter from me to take to the officer in charge of the airport, you will be allowed to go.' How I thanked him. He gave me medication. Whatever it was, in a time like this, it did me good.

In the evening of that day, I spoke with my brother and told him to take my job on the lorry. He refused and said the Germans will tell him where they want him. I told him I pushed myself onto the lorry and it wasn't the Germans who put me there. I took the chance when there was one man missing so he could do the same as I would be leaving there. He would not hear me so it was up to him. I was only trying to help him.

I went into the officer's office next morning, gave him the doctor's letter. He spoke to me ever so nice and in English. I think he felt himself proud to be able to do so. He took my permit away and I asked him if I could keep it with things that I wanted to keep from the Occupation. He let me have it but he said the photo he had to keep and he took it off. So I said 'Good day' and out I went.

Then came again the work problem. I could always fall back on going cutting blackberry leaves for tea etc. Many pounds could be put in sacks if well pressed in. Of course this was only a good weather job. It could not be done in the rain. I took them to people's houses to dry them in their oven. They paid me for them and most seemed to have enough wood etc for heating the oven. There was a nice old couple to whom I delivered, were always cheerful, even to the Germans, but before the end of the war, when the war was won but not ended, the old couple were found dead on the sitting room floor. On the sitting room table was a map of Europe. One can guess for what reason they both were killed, but it was all kept quiet. What could be done when there was no real proof who it was? However no one can be made to stop thinking who it might have been because of that map there. There were still Germans who could not believe that they would lose. I remember once when Hedy and I were at Fermain Bay, we could hear the roar of guns or bombs over in France. It could not be the Germans over England. We were much too close to France. However, Germans not far away from us were talking together and one said to the other 'Can you hear us giving England a real bombing?' We could hardly believe our ears. The Germans must have known how far away England was against the distance to France.

Shortage of Food and Exchanges for Horses' Oats!

With about three Occupation years gone now things started to really get scarce. As the Germans had taken away most of our supplies that they could get to at least we had done really well on what we had, even if it caused us a slow road perhaps to hunger. We thought surely the Red Cross could do something, but my belief is that the Germans did not want to call in the Red Cross as to let them in, Geneva would think the Germans were not looking after us well. However as news was being taken to England by those who escaped, the English knew more than we expected they did. Well as I just said food was very scarce. Bread, our main food was cut down awfully. Three pounds a week for each person and it was made with bean powder and potato to help our little bit of flour. We could not call it real bread anymore. However, Hedy did a bit of housework to help a baker's family at the Old Mill, St Martin's. She thought we had enough to eat until Hedy told her. Then she invited Hedy to a 9 o'clock snack of a piece of bread and coffee.

There was a well-known trio in St Martin's. A butcher, a baker and a farmer. They all looked well, also their families. We don't blame them, but they did not know how badly off we were. Also, soap got to be scarce. Razor blades we could no longer buy. However a Guernsey man found out he could sharpen them which we were very thankful about. Also, Guernsey matches were made, even someone tried soap. All these things were made in Guernsey during the Occupation and were very good to say in what conditions they were made in, and also from what.

Quite a few Black Markets were about. Some pre-war food goods etc were to be seen in their windows. These people were not looked at as decent people, we hoped they would be dealt with afterwards. Cigarettes were the gold at that time. They reached sometimes ten times the real cost. To get food or clothing one had to have cigarettes.

It did not matter what I said to Hedy once you really need some food. I saw advertised that someone was exchanging 5lbs of oats for 40 cigarettes. I said to Hedy I can get rid of my grey flannel trousers and get cigarettes for them. She said you wouldn't have any flannels then but I said food is more important, so I went to one of those Black Market chaps and found out from one and the best deal I could find was 60 cigarettes for my flannels. As I had not smoked for quite a while I kept a few. For the rest I found out I could get oats. I was ever so pleased to go home with my oats but alas when we opened the bag at home they were oats

meant for horses! There was chaff, small pieces of hay, mixed with them. It all had
to be sorted out. Of course we could eat them but we wondered how many horses
had gone short of his or her meal to satisfy this farmer or the Germans' hunger for
a smoke. I hoped this man, whoever he was, or woman whom I doubt, was very
hungry afterwards.

We were soon to learn that we could make a jelly sort of food from seaweed. So
now many went on to the beaches, but as some had been closed by the Germans
we had to have a permit to go to some. However, when we made this jelly it was
a help, but it did not fill us up much. We could go to the chemists and buy it. Of
course it had to be dried first.

It was always a job with the heating fuel. A lot of trees were being sawn down
for the civil population. We had each a ration. To get logs burning sometimes was
a job. We needed bellows or our own wind which was like a hard day's work.
Hedy helped my mother for a time each morning because mum had a weak chest
but to say, she kept up quite well. People also complained that the coal ration took
too long to be delivered. Well, it had to be done by horse or hand cart. I thought
with a lady's bike I could perhaps get coal, two or three bags full, two in the frame
and one on the back carrier. This I tried and I could do it quite well. As time went
on I also had to put a water hose on the front wheel as the tyre gave up and would
not work anymore. I did this for months. People were quite pleased and I received
a lot of tips for my trouble which helped us along.

Salt was also being made from sea water. If cooked in a pan until the water was
all drained off, then a little grey powder salt was at the bottom of the pan. Down
near the castle was the model yacht pond. There was talk about using this as a
place for making salt but it never took place. Possibly the Germans did not want
Guernsey men near the castle as they were fortifying it with guns etc, using a lot
of concrete.

ISLANDERS MADE TO WALK THROUGH THE NIGHT

Some German boats had also been sunk by the RAF. The Germans said some of us
would have to pay for this so the Germans decided that all the English-born people living on the Island would be taken away. They would have to meet at a central
place in a cinema or hall to be examined by a doctor. Of course a lot were not fit
to go, but were still sent off. Some dispute at the harbour took place before they
left. The Germans had sent cargo boats in many cases to fetch these people. One
boat was even said to be a coal boat. The Commandant was called down there.
For once he was quite understanding and said these people did not deserve this,
another boat must be sent. Most of these English people were well-to-do people,
and it was harder for them. The weather was cold so that some ladies had their fur
coats on etc. For some it was a hard taste of the other kind of life. They were taken
through France into Germany. Women and children together, men were sent to
another building in most cases. My writing cannot inform you of this. *One Man's
War* would be the book to read about this.

There also came the time in Guernsey when quite a few of the German telephone cables were damaged. The Germans of course put the blame for this on

the Guernsey people. They forced men to go the whole night long walking along the cables, letting them run through their hands to see if they were still intact. My brother was ordered to go, I did not get the order. For what reason we do not know, but it was not fun my brother said, to be out there in the cold night walking about with this cable running through one's hand. Each man was spaced out so that one had to walk until each reached the other and back again to the other man on the other side. One morning during the day when the men did not have to go, a farmer saw the reason for the cable damage. The cables in many cases were put down too low and along hedges. The farmer's bull was having a fine tackle at the cable of course damaging it. The farmer got in touch with the Commandant at once and told him to come and have a look. He did and was satisfied with what he saw. The men did not have to go anymore.

We would also have had to do a lot of other things that would have not been caused by Guernsey people.

There was a gentleman living in the Havelet Road. He was a real gentleman. He often risked his life for his Island. He knew the international law and very often told the Germans what he knew and understood what could be done to this Island under Occupation. He was, sorry to say, caught himself for having I believe two English soldiers who had come to scout for England and had missed their return ship in the night and were stranded in Guernsey. The soldiers and he were sent to Germany. English soldiers had very often been on the Island in the night looking at German installations in some cases being caught.

There was once a low wall of stones built across Jerbourg Road during the night. The Germans could not drive their lorries along here until of course it was removed. This again was the work of the British army during the night. Anyone who reads this book would say that happened before this or that. That is quite true but at the start, I said dates I would not mention and as you notice I have only mentioned Christian names. What I mention here is the truth. Every page I write is real to someone who was there during the Occupation.

We had moved from a cottage near Luff's Store, St Martin's and gone to live in a nice tiny cottage near the top of Fermain Bay. We also had nice friends as neighbours. Jackie our cat was still with us. She was thin like us but her Persian fur helped to hide this. We expect the Germans did not want her, as she was not fat enough. Many people lost their cats. We ourselves saw Germans with sacks on their backs. Sometimes it could have been another cat.

It was a pity that families had broken up. Some men and women could not take the strain of living alone anymore and some started to live together and in some cases have children. There was going to be a lot of trouble when peace came to us. The friends that we visited were all families that had stayed together, hard as it was, it was better for them.

Tunnels were built everywhere it seemed, where the ground seemed to be a bit higher. We expected they were stores but not one seemed or wanted to say, even the Guernsey chaps who drove or had to drive their lorry for the Germans. However one we knew after a while would be a hospital and ammunition store at St Andrew's under what was called the Chain House.

All the time that the Germans had been here, cars and motorcycles had to be registered so that the Germans just came and got them when they wanted them.

Some of my mates had some lovely motorbikes, they lost them all. In Guernsey there was quite a variety of bikes because the boys always wanted to have something different. They treasured them so much it hurt them really to lose them. My chums sometimes used to come out with cars but those, they belonged to their fathers. My cousin had a lovely Velocette. He took out the piston thinking the Germans would not take it, but they did. We wondered if they ever got a Velocette piston because they never got to England to get a spare! Ronnie, my cousin, never got his Velocette back either.

I knew a bus driver who kept his motorcycle under his kitchen table. The table was made that nobody could notice this box with a bike in. I know through others that he did it, but the kitchen table I never saw. There was also a farmer who had his car under a stack of hay. His car was in a frame built over it then hay put over this. It is said that many Germans had tested that stack with hay forks, but his car was never found. The hay must have been laid on that frame very thick indeed. We knew these little stories were true because the motorcycle and car were seen on the roads and in the town on Liberation Day. They had even kept enough petrol to have a drive about. The locals had a good laugh, but the Germans must have wondered where did those come from?

We had tried to make cars and buses go with coal and wood burned to produce gas for the engine, but this used too much fuel and a bus hardly got up the hills so the idea was given up. So where possible horse buses were used although there was not much to be had in the town. Even people from Pleinmont wanted to come to town. They even managed to come by horse bus a few times. In one case they could have got 2ozs of sweets after perhaps half an hour in a queue. Mind you one-eighth of a pound! Tell you how much value even this was to us. Even to see a few sweets. Queues were seen everywhere. At times I myself missed food by one or two persons. The food had run out before the queue reached me. Even a pound of carrots would have done Hedy good. This was of course when carrots were out of season.

An English battleship was once sunk by the Germans. I believe seventeen bodies or more were washed up on the Guernsey shores. These English sailors were buried at the Foulon Cemetery. We wondered what the Germans would do. However they gave them a decent funeral. The Germans were there to bury them like they said, their comrades in war. They died doing their duty. The workmen said after the burial that German officers were often seen on horse back near the graves, standing there in silence and also giving the English salute. It gave the workmen the idea that at least some of these Germans were gentlemen. Like Rommel of Germany once said 'My friend Montgomery'. He did not mean a loving friend, I don't believe, but a gentleman to be respected because Rommel knew that Hitler was no one to be respected.

The Americans and the RAF bombed the Island at different times. A really sad story was when a German submarine was known to be in harbour. Planes had photographed this. However, instead of doing something that day, they bombed what they thought was the submarine the next day. But it was not there anymore, it had gone off in the night. The town church was damaged, many shop windows were blown out so that we could not go to town for at least half a day, the goods that were lying about the streets had to be collected and taken into the shops again.

The Germans had a plane detector at the corner of the citadel at the fort. They bombed it as they thought but missed by fifty yards at least. From high up perhaps it was not a bad miss. However, in cases like this we said it was the Americans because we believed the RAF bombed better. We as British were proud to believe this, although we were also very thankful to have the Americans helping us now in the war.

A thing that also was hurtful to us was that the Germans in Germany used their churches as factories or stores. Also in Austria the church bells had been melted down to make bombs. It was said, and I believe true, that the church bells of St Anne's in Alderney were taken to France but were not melted down, we do not know why they were brought back again by the British. We expected the Germans believed that the same thing was going on in London because very often churches seemed to be their target. I believe about 360 churches in London were bombed.

Alderney had long been given up as a help for Guernsey food. We had planted a lot there but the Guernsey men told the Germans 'You treat us with your orders like prisoners of war but you only occupy us', so the Guernsey men did not stay in Alderney anymore to the mercy of the Germans. Although the Germans took the best buildings for their use, the best hospital, the best cinemas etc, etc, they did not mix up the Guernsey breed of cow with the ones they brought over from France, thank goodness. They also used a lot of horses, also brought over from France. As time went on there were less about as they were being used for horse meat. We also had rations of meat in this way.

A Tandem Made and it Worked!

It came into my mind to try and make a tandem (a bicycle for two as we say). I had seen one made from two bicycles and had a talk with a bicycle mechanic near the Queen's Hotel, St Martin's about this. I told him how I intended to do it. He said it could not be done, but I thought I must try because we had two really good tyres but not two bikes. So I searched in old iron depots etc, and soon found another frame as I did not want to spoil another good bike. The only trouble was to get the front sprocket of the right kind and distance because on the back frame there had to be two sprockets.

Well, after a while I found a second sprocket and the tandem was soon fixed up and on the road. We did many miles with it and were asked about it. I had painted it a light grey and it looked ever so nice. Hedy had a bit of a job some-times because while I pedalled she had to as well, so once I said you have a try at the front. This she did not like, saying there was too much weight on her arms. Once she said 'The bloomin' thing is mad'. I could ride it alone quite well like another bike, it was not much different. There was a snag again so far as the chain was concerned on the front two big sprockets, however I soon fixed this up with a flat piece of steel fixed to the frame and pressing on the chain like a spring. It grabbed a bit on the chain but, because of oil, we never heard or noticed it. It worked well, took up the slack so that the front chain was always tight. We knew that we could not fly a little English flag on the tandem, but we would have liked to. So we put a little Swiss flag on the front. It was there for months until someone told us to remove it before the Jerries kicked up a fuss. We did as we had been told.

As we could no longer heat our houses properly with open fires I thought of trying out an idea like the Swiss. I got quite a big tin, also searched for a pipe, any would do, even a water pipe if there was one about. After a while this was also fixed up. It looked like this in front of the fire place with a pipe up the chimney.

This warmed our sitting-room in the winter months quite well. Hedy did not miss anything. But me, a Britisher, missed the open flames. All houses in Guernsey had to have black-outs of course, but there was not always cloth to make them so sometimes it was a job with paper and cardboard, which we also needed for fires. Everything was of value. No one will believe, but only those who were there at the time. We could even sell bent screws with damaged heads. Why worry one's mind when everything could be repaired, put straight or used for something? Tin of any kind when thick enough was used to make saucepans, frying pans etc. A visit to a cottage near the forest church has a kitchen of war time Guernsey.

We were now getting a ration each week of saccharin. We had no more sugar. Hedy found a way to make jam as we had some fruit in our garden such as black-berries, etc. We took some to friends, they liked it ever so much that they even wanted to buy some from us. I don't remember if they gave Hedy any sweetening, but she made quite a lot of jam which was enjoyed by all.

We were also told that if we put tomatoes in a box in wood shavings they would keep for a long time. We tried it and after a few weeks we decided to use some. They were quite good but had a not too nice woody smell and taste so we gave up the idea.

The Germans had now for months been working on their own railway. They knocked down houses and walls wherever the rails were, they said they needed to go. Of course ninety per cent of these railways were French made. The tons of cement these railways must have pulled along to make their bunkers will never be known.

BUYING SEA WATER!

The Germans had also closed the beaches and bathing places only leaving what we knew as the men's bathing places were left open. Beach's sea walls were also fenced off with barbed wire. If they had ever known that all this work was for nothing! At least we did not believe that Churchill would invade the Channel Islands before he had France in his power and that this land that the Germans had taken, in two weeks would be all freed again. However, the Germans thought they knew best and, as far as we know, there were 20,000 Germans here in Guernsey that Hitler could have used in France when the invasion would come. So in some way our Islands helped England by having this large number of troops in Guernsey. How many Germans there were in all the islands must have been around 40,000 I should think. Well as I said before, the beaches had been closed to the public so that we could not even go and get shellfish of any kind. A lot of people had used salt water to cook so now there was the trouble getting even this water. Some lorries put tanks on their lorries and a ration of petrol was allotted to them. There was a notice that we could go to different places in the Island and get sea water from these tanks on lorries and of course there were queues. Also the water had to be paid for so much a pint (about ½ litre). Now here we are, the sea water queue, and to believe, paying for sea water! Who would believe it but it is perfectly true! Even living on an Island surrounded with salt water. Even the Germans took to using it. Of course *they* had it free!

My brother Percy now worked at the State's dairy driving a lorry. He looked well, he looked better than he ever had. We knew why, he was well off as far as milk was concerned. Of course the Germans took more than they really needed to take so the Guernsey chaps had a good drink sometimes. I can't prove this but I can just imagine.

However, with all these ups and downs of the Occupation our visits to friends could always be fun as Ronnie's family living at Saints knew. We had many laughs about Hedy's house in Switzerland, because Hedy said her garden had to be made smaller because of lorries which had to pass. There was a while now when we could send Red Cross messages. Just 25 words, but a lot of news was sent over to England because of sentences with two meanings. They took three months to go and to come so that a Red Cross message could say that some relations were quite well but, because of three months coming, these people could be dead by the time the message came. It was very unpleasant in some cases. Hedy lost her youngest brother and mother during the Occupation. We also received the news three months afterwards.

We had a feeling one day and during the night because the dogs barked. During the night and the next day we could hear a lot of planes about. Looking up we

Queuing to buy sea water in the Rohais, St Peter Port

could see like two planes near to each other. We soon were to know that the invasion of France had taken place. The Germans put up notices that we had to behave ourselves and in no way cause trouble to the German forces in their movements. We were always warned that we could be shot for anything. There were now quite a few Russian soldiers in the German army. Prisoners of war who had joined up to get as they believed, more food. Near the Queen's Hotel, St Martin's, one guard held up Hedy and I. Hedy asked him in German what he wanted from us. All he could say was 'Halt' (stop) but talk German he could not as he was a Russian. I must say that these planes flying close together were really gliders being pulled by planes. We were excited then we danced for joy. The Germans must have noticed this.

CRYSTAL SETS HIDDEN IN STRANGE PLACES!

There were some amusing tales told about people who had little radio sets. A man was just listening to his when he saw a German coming towards his door. He had one of those chairs for invalids with the pot in the seat of the chair. He quickly put the radio in the pot and sat on the chair with his pants down! He told the German to come in when he knocked. He was looking for radios. He saw the man sitting there and the man said, 'Excuse me but I get these bouts and with this food we have now, and I get taken like this.' The German excused himself and went out.

Friends of ours were also visited by the Germans for the same reason. The window was a bit open. A German was standing there and without him noticing she pushed the radio out onto the window sill telling him 'It's cold isn't it?' and closed the window. If he had only looked out on the sill he would have seen it. We were lucky that we could make these radios so small!

My brother had owned a little radio set for quite a while now. We needed no batteries, it was just a coil, a crystal, aerial and earth wire. However we had always to find a place to put the aerial in the loft or out of sight. In the end I managed to make one from bits and ends. The earphone was the problem. People with telephones used them for that. However the ones I used, two of them, one for Hedy and one for me, were old German pilot helmet phones. A chum of mine working still at the airport got them for me. How he got them I don't know but I was thankful to have them. From that time on we had something to do when going to bed early because of no gas or electricity. Tommy Handley kept us happy for many hours!

We still had rabbits and I had an idea with the aerial. The cottage was quite low so the aerial in the loft was of no use. The garden was higher up, up a few steps so the aerial was put up over and along the high bush around the garden. The neighbours could not see into our garden, but once a lady saw me putting it up. I had not guessed she would be there. We could not trust anyone we did not really know those days, so I said to her that so many rabbits have been stolen these days that I put up this wire, 'Anyone, German or our people, who try to get over this hedge will come in contact with the wire and a bell will ring in our cottage giving us the alarm.' She said 'what a good idea'! Well, we were going to be very happy now with music etc but it was going to be one of the worst years of the Occupation that we had been through.

It is a new chapter which will have to be started because it is a great pleasure to us in Guernsey that at least we, the Allies, are back in France. We, or Mr Churchill, said we would come back and we have. However for us a pleasure, but for many a sad day as the hundreds of soldiers who lost their lives on these beaches in France will never be forgotten. Five different nationalities all wanting to be free, and free us from the Nazis.

To write about these days that we lived through in the last few months would be hard for me to do. No bread, no light, gas or electricity. No petrol, paraffin or oil. I kept no day book, only my memory, which is very good. I was just an ordinary working man with no means of money to pay Black Market prices. I did buy my wife a little salt for a terrible price and Guernsey matches, which cost an awful price too.

As the weeks went on we wondered if the British would perhaps come sometime in the night and take over, but then in the same thought we would think that the Germans would come back and bomb us. We still believed our British would take us over when the Germans had no chance or means of coming back. The fields had been stripped of all weeds or plants that could be eaten, the beaches were all closed. The Germans also ate something they never believed they would eat: we had heard that in Alderney there was a concentration camp, where most Russians there were eating grass, as there was nothing else whatsoever to eat.

Our troops in France were getting on well, but slowly. The Americans had had a hard start at one of their beaches. However, we British had pulled great concrete portions of the Channel to France. These were hollow and afterwards sunk to the sea bed in France, end to end to form a harbour. Old ships were used also as breakwater against the waves. The Germans had never expected the harbour. They expected the invasion to take place on a beach or beaches, but ship unloading etc would have to take place in a harbour. So Mr Churchill said also 'Good we will take one there'.

Many hundreds of soldiers lost their lives in the swamps which the Germans had made in low lying land near the coast. These men were the parachutists in the night. However every day now we heard of a new place being taken. Even if small, this kept us saying it would not be long now. But for the Invading Troops it was a sad story to know, when on taking some places, to find out that trained soldiers had been fighting against boys of perhaps even 14 years of age. This was Hitler's Second Front. Rommel knew when Hitler told him about his Second Front that Germany had no more real soldiers. If any, they would be kept for Germany itself. The bunkers at the beaches were in many cases manned by foreigners in German uniforms.

We even used to go down to Cobo Chippie. We knew a nice man who used to talk down there, Uncle Willy. My godfather's wife was there sometimes. She was a Sark lady. We don't know why she did not go to Sark to live during the Occupation, as it was said Sark had enough to eat. Sark is almost all farmers and there were not a lot of Germans to feed there. Uncle Willy had a lovely very old farmhouse near Cobo Bay. Near Cobo the Germans had pulled down a lovely house just for the sake of having their rails straight.

Things got worse in Guernsey as far as food and footwear was concerned. The Allies were now in France. The harbours etc were not easy to get in or out of. Of course this could not be helped. Ships came less often. Wonderful work was done on all sorts of footwear. They were made longer at the front of the upper being opened, a bigger toe piece put on and longer sole etc. Of course leather was also short. A good thing for soling shoes was rubber linoleum from bathrooms wherever it was possible to be had. Sometimes auction sales were held. I went to one with my cousin Ronnie C. He had enough money, they were well off. He bought a small packet of Persil washing powder for 30 shillings (150 pence). He said it was something we had not seen for so long, the washing would be clean for once! Of course in many ways it was going back to at least 20 years or more, as we had almost nothing of anything left. It was said that some workmen on the White Rock unloading the boats had their underpants' legs tied around their legs. In this way they used to fill up a part of their underpants with rice etc. I believe some were caught. It was bad for us when some of our police could not keep their hands away from our food stores. The Germans were pleased of this because if food was missed we would of course put it down to them.

A Shooting in St Martins

I remember once for a few weeks I helped with spraying potatoes for the Colorado Beetle that was here sometimes. They came over from France with ships. When I was a boy, we never knew anything about the beetle, but it was found out that it had come to Guernsey. Ever since, we could not get rid of it. This spraying was not a nice job without proper clothes and footwear, especially in the morning when the dew was still on the plants. However, quite near the Foulon Road there was a German family. They had lived there as long as I can remember. Ever such nice people. They were farmers and liked Guernsey ever so much. They were not so liked by Guernsey people just because they were Germans, that's all. However I was spraying their potato fields one morning. At about 9 o'clock the lady called me to come to the house and she told me to come in. She took me into the kitchen, on the table were a few slices of bread and a jug of hot tea or coffee. She told me to sit down and have a meal. While eating this meal she told me she and her family got a bit more food than us because she was German, and also her family. But she told me what the Germans do to one's property makes one's blood boil. She said the Germans on horseback use their fields like a road. They jump over the hedges with their horses into newly planted crops. She said she had been to the Commandant but it made no difference. This lady gave me some bread for Hedy, then again they said at the start of all this occupying, if you respect us we will respect you, well, well!

     Once also at the Hubits quite near where we lived, a farmer's wife getting up early in the morning saw a German soldier in their field. There was broccoli growing there. He was cutting out the middle, just leaving the leaves. She told her husband about it. He at once got his hay fork; he had no rifle or pistol. He said to the German to go off. This Jerry was one who carried an army pistol in his belt. He just fired at the Guernsey farmer who died at once before his young wife's eyes. He himself was about 35. Nothing could be done about it. We heard that the German said that he had acted in self-defence.

Autumn 1944

Now it was going into the autumn of 1944. Clothes were scarce. A shop in the town was advising clothes be made from sheets, blankets etc. I had a pair of trousers made from a light brown blanket. For days something seemed in the way in the seat of the pants. Something kept on sticking me or scratching me and, after a while, I found out it was a pin the young lady who worked on them had forgotten to take out! I went and told her and we both had a good laugh.

My mother laughed about one thing. She said we had to patch the vests over the patch so at least they would be warm! I made myself a shirt once from a curtain, a plain green one. I wore it once or twice even in peace time. I also made myself a zip jacket from a blanket. (Why this happened I do not know because I asked Hedy how to make it before). It turned out in the end when finished that there were two right sleeves. 'Hedy', I said, 'I will have to undo it again.' She said 'No you won't, I will fix that up' and she did. Hedy could mend very well, and could mend socks or anything in wool without anyone being able to see the mend. That was something new for Guernsey!

My father talked to Hedy, but only if he had to because she was foreign. He had quite a bad accident once with a German lorry when he was on his bike. He had to go into hospital and have his head stitched. Hedy was the first one who visited him in the hospital. From then on he was quite different. His workmates said that he talked about Hedy now at work whereas before he had not. We must say that we believe dad was at fault about this accident. He was possibly riding on the wrong side of the road because the Germans had changed it to the right of the road. Also, all our Guernsey roads were numbered for the Germans instead of names. Many years after, in some places this can still be seen.

As the weather got colder there was hardly any gas for cooking or heating when needed. We could get no wood on the cliffs. The Germans were all over there. I was glad when we had a good wind in the night that blew down some branches. I had to go out early then and I went out early as well with the bike around the lanes to see if there were perhaps potatoes growing wild. In this way I used to come home with a few pots or something. I had a garden but only for a short time, on the Fort Road. The States found out that it belonged to someone else who attended it. I never saw anyone attend, however, and I had to leave the crops there. The States gave me a little one for work and crops, but much too little cash.

The Germans had once lived in the house. In the corner of the garden there was still one of their rabbit boxes. It was a sideboard from the house sitting room and the door panels had been knocked out and were nailed there. We heard that the Germans mixed furniture well when they took whatever they felt they liked into their gun posts and bunkers. They knocked, in some cases, rows of cottages all into one.

It got really cold during some nights so that we had a few coats on our bed to keep us warm. Our Jackie was still alive, we wondered how. She also looked for warmth like us. I still had a little petrol, paraffin and oil. We had a small bottle with a tin screw top. I made a hole in the tin and used a boot lace as a wick. We had this little light for months and we could read by it. We went to bed quite early now, read and listened to our little radio. We were very happy then, even if there was so much we needed.

BETTER TIMES AHEAD

There was a big double gate to our house wall leading into the lane. The Germans were on the lookout for people with radios. We would be locked up, or perhaps sent away, so I put a nail in the big hinge of the gate so that it squeaked when it was opened. If anyone was heard coming we put the set quickly out of sight. The RAF came over quite often and we soon heard that leaflets were being dropped. The Germans put up notices that anyone caught going out collecting them would be shot at once! They were in German and were to turn the Germans against his own news. However, we took a chance. Hedy and I went out quite early in the dew covered fields soon after curfew was ended. Hedy was lucky and we found some at different times. With my family standing around, Hedy used to translate them to us. They were a nice little newspaper, even photos of Nazis in France and the Frontier maps. Sometimes they were very wet so we had to take some away from blackberry bushes, ever so easy, and dry them. Some we could not keep, but we kept a few as relics. News always seemed to slip through about something or other unexpected. We had heard that the English people who had to go away to Germany were as well as could be expected. It seemed that they were better off than us in a lot of ways. We had also sent them what we could at different times. It seemed they had formed concert parties, had dances and even fixed up their own 'muratti' (Guernsey versus Jersey). Well, we had sent them football boots etc. All these things had been given to them.

It also seemed that they were receiving Red Cross parcels. Now we asked why don't we? The Germans were told by someone high up that something in this respect should be done. If something was not soon done the Island's population would be in a very bad way, a serious condition if things were left to go on. However the time came along towards Christmas 1944 saying that a ship would come. A Red Cross ship with food and medical supplies for the invalids. The Germans published a date and said that all children should be kept away from school or have the day free to go and see the Red Cross ships arrive. Well we don't know what went wrong, however, the ships were never seen. Many, many eyes looked out to sea on that day but it was a sad day for us. We did not know if it was, once again, the Germans up to a very bad thing. The children, at least, were upset. We think there was some excuse about mistake of dates or something. However it was said that the BBC had even mentioned that the Swedish ship *Vega* would be home for Christmas. However we had not heard it so we did not know. However Christmas 1944 we were given 6 ozs of beef each, 6 ozs of rice, a little cheese and cooking fat. On the morning of December 27th, 1944 a ship was seen out between Herm and Jethou. People who had good eyes to see well could see this big Red Cross painted on the side of the ship. It was the Red Cross ship at last!

There was now to be some trouble about berthing her. The Germans would on no condition allow her to be berthed elsewhere as to where they wanted her. The Guernsey Harbour Master told them she was an old ship and to put her near the fruit export sheds on the careening hard side would not be a good spot. The bottom of the harbour there is not flat and she would be damaged at low tide. Of course the Red Cross gentleman from Geneva, Switzerland had no power against these Nazis so the boat was berthed where the Germans said she had to be. There, or not at all. So she was put there.

She was supposed to call about every month. Leaving here she would go to Lisbon in Portugal, load and then return. Of course, calling at Jersey after she had unloaded her Guernsey share. However because of the Germans and their stubbornness the ship did not return for six weeks. She had had to have an overhaul in Portugal. They said it had not done her keel any good in Guernsey, being berthed in the wrong place.

Gas and electricity were now fading out. We lived now like the birds, up or awake with the daylight and going to bed with the dark. However, we had a little bit more in our cupboard. The parcel was about twice as big as a shoe box. There was egg powder, chocolate, sugar, a nice sized tin of meat etc. There were some Canadian parcels and also New Zealand parcels, all with the Red Cross signature and Geneva on them. They were a godsend. As there was hardly any bread now, I used to have a spoon of condensed milk in the morning and Hedy a slice of bread as she was worse off than I was. I usually used to go off scouting for food or cutting blackberry leaves. There were sometimes broccoli leaves to be had at the markets or a sort of spinach with a wide white stem. We were told when we fried these white stems it was almost like bacon. Well, how other people's imaginations were allowed to run, but it doesn't matter now. It all helped a little, in a tiny corner of our stomachs.

During this Occupation, knitting had been the main hobby and all sorts of old wool was used. Some people told us that there were parcels for people who were

Extract from a newspaper Frank retrieved from the fields

Drawing by Bert Hill, a printer and well-known artist, working for The
Star *newspaper, kindly loaned by Mrs Sims*

not too well. They called them invalid parcels, and we could apply for them, so
we did and we got invalid parcels each. I am not sure now but I believe the ordinary parcels had cigarettes or tobacco for the men, whereas the invalid parcels did
not as not so few women smoked then, so they did not need them. However, the
invalid parcel was better for some of us.

It also got around something unbelievable that some people had been known
to sell some Red Cross goods for a high price or put some in the Black Market
shops. However, it was soon to be seen in the local newspaper that anyone found
doing this would not receive anymore Red Cross parcels. The contents of these
parcels were really helpful, but to make them last a month needed a good will.
People were asking each other 'have you still got some left?' after even a few
days. We would have liked to eat our parcels a lot quicker but this would have
been of no use. Also, we did not know if we would always get the parcels each
month. After the first we had to wait six weeks because of the ship being held up
for inspection.

Time went slowly on and we were always looking for the end to all this. Many
Germans were as well. Hitler gave up giving his speeches, and they knew it was
looking black for them. They ought to have known by now that they had been
told in many cases a bundle of lies. Mr Churchill always said 'We don't want to

The Vega *with a guard ship (Richard Heaume)*

get rid of the Germans, we want to get rid of this 'Nazi thinking' in Germany. This mass murder of people (Jews) can't help you.'

We did not know that before the Liberation came we would be without bread for five weeks long. Our main food was bread and we were told we would soon be without any. However, we got in touch with the Red Cross and it was said that the *Vega*, the Red Cross ship, would bring on one of its trips a cargo of flour. We had also been a while without bread before this arrived. The Germans wanted to give us some of their flour until ours came, when we would have to give it back in tons when the Red Cross flour arrived. Although it was hard for us to be without bread for long, we refused to take the German flour because the German flour was more like cement than flour. I know this because I worked for a short while for the mills at the Charroterie. We had to crush German flour with the crusher! It was given to local people as pudding flour. It was awful stuff, must have been quite old and was grey. If we had taken this in exchange for Red Cross flour it would have been awful. The Germans knew what they were up to. However, when the flour did arrive the Germans offered their steam train to transport our flour to store at 'Braggs'. It must have hurt them to see all this lovely white flour, but they had hurt us many times. We had done them no bodily harm but they had been cruel to us in many ways.

We noticed though that the Nazi salute was not used so much on the roads now as it used to be. Very often when the RAF paid us a visit the whole island was lit up with lights which they dropped. I forget the real name (flares?). One could read a newspaper they were so bright! Planes bombed the Fort once. They were supposed to be American planes and it was said that, at the time, a lot of Germans were up there. We found a bullet shell in our garden, quite a big one and someone said they were from what was called 'cannon fire', not machine guns.

FRANK AND HEDY'S LIBERATION

However we had pushed on into Germany and that country had to give in with the push of the Russian Allies on the other side. I danced when I heard Mr Churchill say 'Tomorrow our dear Channel Islands will be free.' I called Hedy and said 'Listen', but he only said it once.

We expected some noise in the night but it was as peaceful as could be. At six o'clock in the morning I could stay in bed no longer. I got up and went down towards the town. I could have looked out from the top of George Road near the fort field, but I did not know what to expect. I got down as far as the top of Cornet Street and went onto the plateau there, that was enough for me. All I could see were ships between Herm, Jethou and Guernsey. A man told me it was all over. We received a special newspaper saying we were free and that we could put up flags at dinner time. But people could not wait. As I walked, or ran, home to Hedy, flags were already out and I told Hedy to get up and dressed, then we would go and see the sights.

The Americans and English knew we were in a bad state but they never expected to see us so well-dressed. Many people, well almost everyone, kept their best clothes for this day. Old half-broken footwear was polished. The white shirts were from sheets. Hedy had French war-time shoes all polished up. Her green costume she could get on easy as she was quite thin now. I always kept my black suit for special days etc. I was no bigger than when I was seventeen when I had this suit. There were many like us and we wanted to look nice, at least for this day.

Well, when we got down there a huge American landing ship was blocking the entrance of the old harbour. Lorries and motorcycles were being driven out of its open bows. The water and tide where down and the sea bed had been covered with

Viva flour being unloaded at Mr Bragg's store. Photograph taken from window at No 21 Esplanade (Mrs E. Orr)

iron netting so as to make a firm footing for the lorries loaded with food etc. Many lorries and jeeps and motorbikes had the names of their sweethearts or wives painted on them. The drivers and riders gave us the 'thumbs up' sign. About twenty-five British soldiers marched up and down. They were the first that had landed to take over Guernsey from the Jerries. The British and Americans were all ready to take over Guernsey by force but this was not needed, the Germans gave in after a bit of trouble when in the night they had sent the wrong man to sign the surrender. In the end the right one came, but it was touch and go for a few minutes on the HMS *Bulldog*. They said if the Germans did not soon come to sign we would fight.

There were also a lot of 'ducks' in the harbour. They were a British invention and they ran on land and could swim like a duck. Quite near the Ship Inn steps a British soldier came out of a duck with perhaps six 2lb loaves under his arm. I believe he only did this to see what we would do. I grabbed one and he laughed but I was not to have all of it long, a boy grabbed the other end so I let him have half. All day long the Americans had been throwing packets of all sorts on land, cigarettes, soap, sweets etc. We wondered how many arms went up that day catching all these goods we had not seen for so long and they were free! We went home that night well pleased with ourselves. With one or two slices of bread, a little radio music from the now not forbidden radio. A piece of bread for Blackie and perhaps a glass of warm water or condensed milk. What could we wish for then? We were at peace. Goodnight, sleep well. Tomorrow we will go and see the sights again.

I believe we did this for three days. Someone said the troops said 'Don't these people ever go home?' There was a parade with the Manchester Regiment Band, our Legion Soldiers, and veterans of the First World War. We were there as they marched down the Grange. The Liberation Speech was given on the steps of Elizabeth College. Whoever reads the book would think the last few weeks had gone quickly, but at the time of writing I still can't fathom how we managed to keep so well as we did. The doctors said it was because the fresh vegetables, even if only leaves sometimes, had kept us alive. Illnesses in peace time were often caused by the preparing and colouring of bought food, however we were overjoyed to see some food in packets again.

I got a job as a postman. I did not have a uniform, just a band on my arm. I had a permit to go on to the New Jetty to help with the post. Some that we really needed at that time were allowed also but I could not understand that at that time relations and near friends were kept behind a barricade at the Weighbridge clock, while some were allowed to go right up to the boat's gangway. We don't know who organised this, but after a few months people of all classes were allowed to go. My post round took me near and around St Jacques. I liked the job but my turn was not long enough, so that I could not keep this on for ever, as a married man I needed more hours.

With Hedy's health and no sign of a little one I said we ought to try and get up to Switzerland. The doctor had also told my mum, 'if only we could get you over to Switzerland for a while, you would be better'.

The post had a lot of work as the shops started to order goods by post. Big cardboard boxes for shoe shops etc, perhaps with 10 pairs in or more. I got Hedy a lovely pair of shoes from a shop. This was her second pair because at first the woman who needed shoes had been issued with girl's army shoes. These were

Landing craft in the old harbour, now the Victoria Marina (J. Priaulx)

lovely and were very strong. However, as time went on this overweight post was stopped and the goods had to come by the usual transport. A lot of people had made themselves rich because of the Occupation, such as Black Market shop organisers. However, they were reported and kept back. They thought they would buzz off at once and leave the Island, but that was not the case.

THE KING AND QUEEN ARRIVE

After a few weeks of peace the king and queen visited the Channel Islands. It was like father and mother coming home! We felt ever so well, really not forgotten. We were glad to be a part of the British Empire, now the Commonwealth. We were taken well care of after the German Occupation. We cheered as they went along the different streets and roads of Guernsey and I am sure we could have cheered louder, but we were so taken up with all the goings on. These two people had also walked the streets of bombed London and other towns, talking and comforting people. Like the Liberation Troops they also were surprised to see children and grown-ups so well-dressed. But like I said before, we kept all these nice things for a day like this. There used to be a saying, and we still hear it sometimes, 'clothes make a person'. My mum, like a lot of other mums, said 'You need not look posh and perhaps you have not such nice clothes but you need not have dirt or holes.' So we believed everyone at that time did their best to look nice. People like Ronnie's family from Saints Road did wonders in this way, thanks to their dear old mum and dad. There were many like them but we think people like them should get a medal as we say. To bring through this Occupation a family with children was no

The crowd greet the Liberation Forces (Richard Heaume)

joke. We had hoped that Mr Churchill would visit us but it was said he was over-taxed with work or it would not be safe. We do not know. However he sent us his best wishes and thanks for our wishes for his well being.

Now to Switzerland!

After a few months we left for England, our first leg of going to Switzerland. One of Hedy's relations had died and left us a little so we decided to go. Hedy and I got jobs as chauffeur-valet and cook in a lovely villa once lived in by Winston Churchill. I would not believe this and I believed my boss was boasting. However it was true and he proved it to me at Hascombe Farm. Hedy got taken really ill and had to go to a clinic in Guildford. The English doctor who came to the villa told her she should go back to Switzerland, but we could not go because I was British, though Hedy could have gone. However, I went to London to visit the French and Swiss Consulates and they told us 'not yet'. We told them once on the telephone that Hedy had also lost her mother and brother during the time of the Occupation and also what the doctor said and after a while we were told that we could go. We would have a visa for three weeks' stay which could be lengthened to two weeks longer. It was not very hopeful, but we took the chance and we returned to Guernsey in March 1946 for a holiday before leaving for Switzerland.

We arrived in Mosle, Switzerland just under a year after Liberation. I must say we were the first passenger ship (British at that) to go from Guernsey to St Malo since the war. The gentleman who had gone to France to get us food etc was aboard. For once I will use his name, Mr R.O. Falla. We have to thank him for a lot, and all who helped him in his, sometimes unbelievable, task because he was always under German control. He had no free hand in France, otherwise we would have been better off.

Just before I close I want to say that some people we have met who were in Guernsey during the Occupation said they had enough to eat. 'How did they do this?' we wondered. They know, we don't. We only know that when Guernsey had applied to the Red Cross the local doctors had said that Guernsey was at the point of starvation, they did not mean a few they meant most of us, so how these people could have more than others is nothing to be proud about. However, thank God to all who helped the needy in every way. They deserve something that money or a medal can never repay.

PS – We were allowed to stay in Switzerland. We enjoyed very much our stays in Guernsey and England during holiday time. Home from home both ways, we get homesick for both places. We have now a daughter, Heidi.

Alf Le Poidevin's Memoirs

I had many conversations with Alf Le Poidevin as he was a good friend of mine and my husband, André. Many a time we met at La Vallette Pools where Alf swam every day until he decided to stop (because of age and ill health); he would talk of his dealings with the Germans and his frights! Alf and Eileen (his wife) enjoyed over 60 years of married life, and together must have shared a similar time to Frank and Hedy, being a young married couple also occupied. Sadly, both have now passed away but before Alf died, together we wrote his memoirs.

Alf Le Poidevin began working as a driver for the firm of W. Head and Son in 1934. He remembers very well the duties he was asked to perform at the beginning of the German occupation of Guernsey in 1940.

Firstly he helped with the evacuation of the RAF from the airport to the harbour because they had priority in leaving the Island before the Island evacuation of others. He writes of the terrible mess after the German air raid on the harbour when 34 civilians were killed, 50 injured and lorries burnt out on Friday 28 June 1940. On Saturday 29 June the air raid sounded again, he had been sent to the State's offices – it was 'panic stations' with everyone diving for cover under desks etc. After the 'all clear', work began again but because of the State's offices' position, everything (papers etc) had to be loaded and moved inland, to Saumarez Park, the authorities fearful of more air raids on the harbour. It was a worrying time for everyone and it was on the Sunday 30th June in the afternoon when Alf and his very good friend, the late Percy Bougourd, saw the very first German plane land also at the airport. Peering through the hedge they also saw the very first Germans walking across to the airport building. Soon everyone would know they were on the Island, they came by air and sea. Alf mentions no sleep and worrying that night, wondering what the future held.

Monday morning, back at work the few remaining drivers were discussing what would happen next. The late George Head who had taken over the firm was trembling as he spoke to the drivers. 'They have phoned from the Royal Hotel saying we want five lorries at the hotel now or we are coming to fetch them and the drivers!' George Head then said 'I am not telling you to go, I am in the same boat as you.' Alf remembers this conversation and these words very well, and after a short discussion with the other drivers, although hesitant, decided it was better that they go.

Alf Le Poidevin

On arrival at the Royal Hotel (situated near the harbour) the men were met by two German officers and told them the mess at the White Rock (harbour) had to be cleared. This was not going to be pleasant but they began the task. Thousands of burnt out trays with which tomatoes had been waiting to be shipped to the mainland had been bombed and were left lying along the quay with burnt out remains of lorries. The trays were placed on the lorries and a trail of tomato juice was left all the way along the sea front to Bulwer Avenue. Because the camber of the roads were leaning to the landside and seeing the roads were not cleaned, by October, tomatoes were growing all along the roadside in the gutter.

Growers, drivers, painters, bus drivers etc, workers had to report to various places and enlist for their trades. Driving was now on the right side of the road. Work started to build bunkers, stone was gathered from La Miellette and

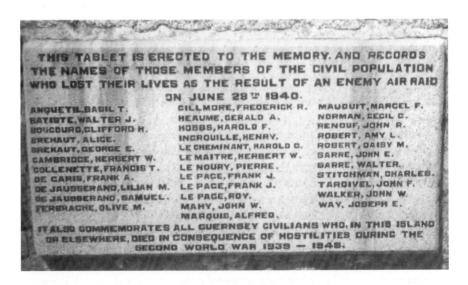

Tablet dedicated to those who lost their lives from an enemy air raid, 28 June 1940

taken to Falla's crushing machines. Best'v s quarry was also working and sand was gathered at various pits such as L'Ancresse and Port Soif for construction work at Jerbourg Point. There were convoys of lorries on the go and roads were very busy.

During the five years of occupation, Alf and other drivers were sent to work at different parts of the Island. Orders were issued by officers in the morning at this time from the headquarters at Elizabeth College. Whilst at the White Rock Alf had an argument with a German guard as to who was going to do the driving – they ended up fighting on the floor! However Alf came off the worse and ended up the passenger. Until 3 pm in the afternoon not a word was spoken between them. Then suddenly the German burst out laughing and held out his hand and they shook hands in a friendly manner, although this German had been sent to stop the stealing etc. What Alf didn't know was that he was no better than the civilian drivers, he never missed anything he could lay his hands on, especially if it was from the German forces. This suited Alf and others I am sure!

THE FIRST OF MANY FIGHTS!

Quite opposite was an O.T. officer who became known as Bullneck – Alf writes 'He was a terror – a brutal man with the workers. He in turn stopped me and ordered me back to load cement. I replied "I am working on the shelter" – out came the revolver into my ribs. I didn't argue with that! I heard later from one of the foreign workers that the worker also lost his life in that action!'

Cruelty and hardship continued for the slave workers. There was one morning Alf was on his way to collect his lorry from Doyle Motors when he met a squad of Germans marching, headed by an officer. There was no singing, which was most unusual. In the middle of perhaps 15 or 18 was one bare-headed soldier, dressed in civilian clothes. Alf realised this could be the one thing one would read about but not witness. As the soldiers marched down glum faced towards the Bouet and then into Pitronnerie Road, he watched them go down the lane heading towards the open quarry by the track (later to become Tektronix) and therafter 'Bowl'. Later a chat with a Mr Duquemin, who was in a stable working for Mr Percy Ash, confirmed Alf's beliefs as he saw the squad returning without their prisoner. He too confirmed this unforgettable scene.

Alf and the drivers of 'Head' and lorries in William Bird coal store, also the Paragon Garage and Blue Bird were all sent to the gun emplacements and bunkers where they met with the foreign workers who were badly treated.

One day Alf was going up St Julian's Avenue when he thought he saw a bundle of rags in the gutter. On closer inspection, it turned out to be a Frenchman. He appeared to be very ill and then told Alf he lived in the camp at the Vauxbelets – wooden huts outside the college gates. Alf bundled him in the cab and set off for Les Vauxbelets, then partly carried him in where an O.T. grabbed him and dragged him inside. Being a little concerned and thinking about him, Alf decided to enquire about the lad when passing the following day. The answer Alf received was a boot in his chest and up his backside on the ground!

Head's lorry adjacent to the Guernsey airport terminal building (J. Priaulx)

Soon after this incident whilst he was driving by the States Offices, he was held up at gun point again. This was by an O.T. who ordered Alf to take him and a Frenchman to the O.T. prison (later being the Iron Stores). On arrival the O.T. got out from the back of the lorry with his prisoner and banged on the door – out came a black man (another O.T.) and grabbed the prisoner throwing him on the floor. (What happened later Alf did not know and many of us will never know all the cruelty that went on in the Islands).

A Shooting and Alf up to Court

Sadly, Alf did have news that his cousin Bertie Jehan had been shot by Germans whilst chasing the soldiers who were digging up his potatoes. He died about an hour later and his funeral took place at the Emmanuel Baptist church which was attended by the Bailiff of Guernsey and Jurat Leale – Alf did notice that two German officers were present.

Life went on and work carried on. Alf was still working at the White Rock when another guard was put on the lorries and this particular one was on Alf's lorry who kept talking all day in German which Alf found strange to be so talkative. However about 4pm he said in perfect English 'you are driving well and you understand German well.' Alf asked him where did he learn to speak English? His answer was 'At university in the USA and in England.' His mother was Japanese, his father German and he spoke nine languages! Alf realised he was a disguised officer spying on the locals and was put on the lorries for a reason, (we also had one at our school and in later editions were written in *A Child's War*).

There was a nasty incident which occurred when a motorcycle ridden by a German corporal collided into Alf's lorry whilst he was parking at the Weighbridge and with a van parked nearby. Alf could not understand why he was being blamed for the accident and it meant endless questioning. He was locked up for two hours afterwards, then again the following morning for four hours at the Albion Court. All was forgotten for two months, then he and a local police

Sergeant, the late Charlie Le Lebvre, was ordered to appear in court (Military Tribunal at 9.00 hours). After a sleepless night he was met by the late Sergeant Dyson who whispered that he didn't know why Alf was there. He was ushered into court by two German guards where nine court officers were also present. It was a long drawn-out session – Germans coming in and out with many 'Heil Hitler's' (Alf excluded) all the time. At long last with a German interpreter 'Mr Le Poidevin' (Alf) was called to the front to address the court and to explain how the accident happened. Alf really thought the worst, as he understood now that the German corporal had lost a leg in the accident. After a court hearing of 2¾ hours, Alf was able to convince the court that the van driver involved had exercised all care and the motorcyclist had been travelling far too fast. Case dismissed! The court thanked Alf for giving his clear evidence and the van driver and the corporal also gave thanks. The corporal was then sentenced to prison for three months. A German in charge called Ernst Bessner replaced the victim of the motorcycle accident (whose name was Carl Kunns). *He* would keep guard while they listened to the news on *his* wireless set. Alf thought, a good man. Every so often the German officer whom Alf and his mates christened 'Donald Duck' would lecture them and say they were like German soldiers and would be treated like soldiers (a correct army!). Alf said to his mate Bill 'Did you hear that, means we can go into the soldaterheum (Naffi) for food!' So a few days later they were out with stone and passing the Carlton Hotel (Naffi) which at the time was painted with a Red Cross to look like a hospital, they knew the opening time was 4pm, so decided to join the queue with the soldiers. At the counter they ordered the same as them – coffee, bread and honey. After three days Alf and Bill were thrown out much to their disgust!

Mirus Battery Gun Emplacement camoflagued to look like a bungalow (Richard Heaume)

As work carried on from the south side they were in charge of Jacob, an Austrian who was a bit of a character. There was no work this particular day being Whit Monday. Donald Duck (the German so called by the men because his bottom was so close to the ground and he quacked like a duck!) issued the order he was coming to inspect the lorries. On inspection he ordered Alf and the others to thoroughly clean the engines and to clean them with petrol. The first lorry was taken outside and work commenced, then whoosh! It caught fire. Two Germans then grabbed a fire extinguisher, rushed out and banged it on the floor, nothing happened! 'Direct sabotage' they said, little did they know that Bill Bennett and Alf had emptied it down the drains a few weeks before, a little espionage by Alf and Bill Bennett eh? These small efforts were done quietly by many all around the Island but it was too difficult with repercussions to do anything major.

With no wireless sets, a big question amongst the men was how to make a crystal set? The small crystal sets proved a great success to hear the daily news. On asking around they soon found out – by using an empty rifle cartridge case filled with lead, zinc and sulphur, by squeezing the end in a vice and placing on the primus stove in the middle of a garage floor, then shutting the door and waiting outside for the big bang!

When the dust had cleared one would have to search for the crystal, sometimes so small and difficult, but it was worth the trouble just to know what was happening in the war.

Fish and Potato Rationing and a Near Miss

As I have mentioned before, families and people living in the St Peter Port had less in the way of food than the country folk. Alf had a nice garden and grew mainly sugar beet for syrups and vegetables. At low tides when permitted he would gather ripe carrageen moss. It was washed and laid out to bleach – eventually becoming white and useable for cooking. At one time, rationed potatoes were 90lb per head for the year, but these allowances altered from time to time. The Germans always had to receive a large percentage of what was grown and available at the depot.

The same applied with fish – fishing was only allowed at certain times and the fishing boat always had a German guard on board. Alf said it was distressing to see people following the cart loaded with crabs going from the boat to the 'Queens weights' to be weighed ready for the Germans to take their large share. What was allowed was taken to the market where a queue was always waiting. Alf's sister Ruth had a market stall but one needed coupons for crabs, one medium spider crab was equal to 14oz of meat allowance. Alf became a member of a boat, *GU88* – and he was really sad as he saw first-hand how much was going to the enemy forces. Once he and his friends decided to go to Jethou to gather limpets for bait as all the beaches were closed to the Islanders at the time. Having moored the boat and the dingy, they were terrified as shells landed above in the bank, sending stones and gravel around, and with shells landing very near the boat, 'That was a near one!' Alf wrote.

There was a day when permission was given when Islanders were allowed on particular beaches along Les Banques, Salerie and Havelet. This particular incident was at Richmond Corner when with a good low tide Alf decided to go for a few ormers (a favourite shell fish amongst us) when a lady came up most stressed and said that a b – – German had come up, taken her basket and tipped her precious catch back into the sea. Alf reassured her he wouldn't do it again and for her to get more and stay nearby and place her ormers in his basket. With sharing the catch, the lady went home happy.

At this time, food was very scarce. Many thefts occured near Alf's house; two heifers were killed one night and a greenhouse of potatoes dug the same night. In the market there was virtually nothing to buy, but there were always hopeful shoppers hanging around to see if any goods would be coming in.

Alf (and Eileen his wife) lived just outside the main St. Peter Port town and there was a time when a lot of activity was going on at the bottom of their lane. 3 x 500lb bombs had dropped nearby, with one only dropping 30 or so feet from Alf's neighbours' back door. The neighbours – husband, wife and children moved in with Alf and Eileen for six weeks until safe to return.

At the airport were 90–100 fighter planes (M/SS109.6) spread out. The following day, all saw the sky black with bomber planes arriving in from France. The fighters then left to go on bombing raids to Plymouth and the South, which were later heard about on the radio.

From Grandes Rocques, explosion after explosion could be heard. The fighter planes returned and the bombers made back to France. This was reported day after day – sadly for many and a worry for the locals to see.

Because Alf was literally amongst the Germans and having to work for them throughout the five years of occupation he was held at rifle or revolver point *five times*! Because his knowledge of the German language was good, he would stand up to them and argue his point of view, but he did wonder how he managed to get away with what he had done and said! He was very lucky indeed.

Queuing in the Pollet for food

WHO'S FOR ALDERNEY?

Some 20 to 30 Men Wanted for Salvage Expedition

It seems quite possible that, in a few days from now, an expedition of Guernseymen will sail from Guernsey for a few weeks' work there in the salving of island stores.

The proposition regarding this work is one that was made to Guernsey's Labour Department, directed by the Controlling Committee of the States of Guernsey, by the German Commandant here, and it was taken up at once by Deputy R. H. Johns, and by the Rev. P. Romeril, who is acting as Mr. Johns' personal secretary, unpaid.

Interviewed this morning, Mr. Romeril said that he could not resist the thought that it had been a mistake to evacuate Alderney completely from the civic point of view. Rather, he thought, should a maintenance staff have remained there to keep things in an orderly way, and to generally watch over the interests of the evacuated Island.

With regard to the proposed expedition, some 30 men of a reliable type would be required, and it was hoped to have that number ready in two days from now. These should register with Mr. P. Honey at the Labour Bureau, States Office, North Esplanade, and the men forming the expedition would be selected from those registering for this.

The Rev. P. Romeril, who is the Methodist Minister at St. Sampson's, and is doing such valued work with Deputy Johns, was in France for five years in the last war, serving in the 55th Division, and was with the Army of Occupation in Belgium and district, and, in the course of his duties, had frequently to go in and out of Germany.

ALDERNEY MEN VOLUNTEERS?

Mr. Romeril observed that there were a number of Alderneymen in Guernsey, and the Authority would be glad to have their assistance in the work contemplated.

Such men could obtain an interview with Deputy R. H. Johns, at Elizabeth College, either to-day or to-morrow.

SARK'S NEW

Bill Martel's Memoirs

Bill Martel, Alf Williams and Bill Gillingham were all young single men in 1940 – hence they have stories to tell!

Bill Martel was a brother-in-law of Alf Le Poidevin and Alf suggested that he also would be willing to record with me his memories. I am pleased I met him before he passed away and went to see him several years ago.

Bill was 20 years of age in 1940 and learning his trade as a carpenter but at this time, there was no work in the building trade so he took up a job in glasshouses.

Then early on, just after being occupied, different groups of men were from time to time offered the chance to go and work in Alderney. Being single and young, he felt it might be a challenge to work there and besides, the pay was better – paying 30 Reichmarks a week! At that time, the rate was 7 Reichmarks to the pound.

Bill Martel

Alderney had evacuated almost all of the population in 1940 but the Island needed help to dig a heavy crop of potatoes, general clearing up and getting houses ship-shape once more. Apparently, many had been ransacked and there was much to do all over the Island. (At the end of the war, the people of Alderney returned to find much damage. Property boundaries were altered, rusty barbed wire everywhere, ruined farms and bunkers filled with water, demolished houses and everywhere infested with rats. Destruction all over the Island. Much heartache was felt I am sure. One can only imagine that the Sark population must have felt relieved that they had stayed on their Island, as they could have also found the same damage and destruction on returning home).

When men were needed, Mick Falla (Bill's boss) approached him and others to ask if they would be willing to go for a few weeks. They agreed and he joined a party of 25 who were met by a German General and marched up to Belview Hotel. Three men out of the 25 were to cook and sleep next door to the kitchen so Bill, with the other two, took up the challenge of different work. He and a colleague stripped the bed and what a shock they had – a large rat jumped out and there were fleas all over and in the bed. Not a good start for him and the others! Anyway, he had to get down to cooking. The potatoes they had were very watery because they had been in the ground for so long. Not very nice but they had a glut of rhubarb so he had to find recipes – stewed, baked, boiled etc. They had to feed the local group (not Germans) which was just as well as one day one of the men found a tin marked 'flour' and they made a cake, but it turned out to be plaster of paris!

Bill said he found life weird on the Island. One family lived there during the Occupation and it was only when he heard children's voices laughing and footsteps running in the town one day did he realise what he had been missing. It was a wonderful sound to him.

April 22nd 1941. When Bill returned to Guernsey, he worked on a farm and had to milk cows – 15 of them! He was pleased as he was rewarded with one and a half pints of lovely full cream milk to take home every day. German inspectors kept an eye on the farmers and checked to see amounts of milk tallied from day to day. No chance to fiddle much. Cows were milked by strangers at night and seeing many Germans were billeted all around the district, it was felt it was them helping themselves and stealing what they could.

Bill felt he was lucky to stay alive after one escapade. It was 9pm and just on curfew time when a guard stopped him and asked to see his Identity Card. The Officer spoke English and told him to carry on after seeing the card, but the German with him decided otherwise and started to follow him. Bill then heard a click of his rifle which almost frightened him to death. He soon got on his bike and peddled like mad out of his way! He knew the German had been drinking and anything could happen. He knew how cruel some could be having seen poor foreign workers in the Rue Sauvage where many were living in terrible conditions. He had seen four placed in a barbwired circle and made to run around whilst a German O.T. in charge would be in the centre whipping them. His uncle had also seen and witnessed the workers thrown in a shed and kept there for four days in L'Islet.

At L'Islet there was also a soup kitchen for the foreign workers but all they were given was watery soup. They were indeed starving with no footwear (just sacking with string tied around) little shabby clothing and yet had to work on building fortifications, tunnels, the railroad etc.

It was difficult for both Alf and Bill to understand how Germans treated the foreign labourers in such brutal ways when at intervals, local lads were allowed to go swimming with them at the Old Harbour Slipway and the gents' pool at La Vallette. Islanders were left alone (if they behaved themselves).

When bathing and beaches were out of bounds, Bill and his friends who normally would all swim together at Rousse Pier, wouldn't be beaten and although the water was jolly cold, would meet and swim in a quarry at Les Amarreurs.

Liberation Day eventually came and although Bill was happy and excited and wanted to get down to St Peter Port, he still did his normal hours of farm work because, like he said, 'he was so grateful for what the cows had given to the population throughout the five years'. He felt proud as punch this day because he placed a red, white and blue rosette on each and every cow to celebrate! What a sight that must have been, but he just didn't know where or how he got those rosettes.

Foreign workers with guards (J. Priaulx)

O.T.s the Organisation Todt worked and guarded the Russians and foreign slave workers in Guernsey

Alf Williams

Alf Williams's Memoirs

I had the pleasure of meeting Alf Williams recently and I knew he had an interesting story of his time when a young man, as I had heard his account at a meeting of the Channel Islands Occupation Society. At the beginning of the Occupation, Alf was one of 400 men who were ordered to work at the airport. Their job mainly was to build hangars for 12 aircraft, the Messerschmitts.

He was working there for four years and during this time, he felt he had done a little for the war effort. He said four Messerschmitts came in to land one day and three out of the four crashed! Secretly very pleased with himself because he had made holes in the landing strip – hence the crashes! He is convinced he caused this although nothing official has ever been recorded by the Germans (naturally they wouldn't)! Anyway at the time he was very proud at what he had done and had put these aircraft out of action. With many planes coming and going at the airport apparently many crashes did occur.

Whilst working there, he was offered other work and a different job, but the Germans refused to release him. After much persuasion to higher authorities, he was eventually allowed to leave and happy about leaving. Alf was aged 19 in 1940, hence he and his pals would get up to a little excitement from time to time. One night his mate suggested they go out on a motor bike as he had managed to get some petrol – so on they jumped and drove to L'Eree passing ammunition dumps where guards were on duty. This midnight ride after curfew could have had serious consequences and they could both have been shot. Alf always thought the guards assumed the two of them were also German and let them go by.

There was another instance just on curfew time when he and his mate were singing together in the road. There was a shout 'HALT!' then immediately Alf felt a revolver in his stomach. There were two Germans and luckily one was more friendly! He grabbed the revolver and threw it over the wall and shooed them both off. The other German had been drinking and things could have turned nasty but for the intervention.

This other time was a morning scare. Alf had a pistol thrust in his back and again the cry 'HALT!' Turning around, he knew the German concerned and said 'What the hell do you think you are doing?' The German quickly replied 'Sorry Willy, we are looking for the troops who have landed.' The Germans were certainly on the

A Messerschmitt 109

look-out, with thousands of the Germans on guard at this time. Another lucky escape for this young Alf.

This is not an incident that refers to the Germans being nasty or stealing but an Islander who also wanted his share of goods! A friend, Roy Machon, suggested to Alf 'Let's raid a store in the Charroterie of German goods!' Although manned by four armed guards, they got in and stole cigarettes, butter, cigars and other items but lo and behold to their surprise, a Guernsey man was waiting for them and said he wanted them to hand over half of all they had or else! He apparently had watched and guessed what was happening and demanded some. Not a nice story but it happened and they had to share.

The V-signs

Like many other Islands, little acts of resistance were carried out and Roy Machon and Alf made V-sign badges between 1942 and 1945. It was a common sight to see V-signs in many different places – locals would chalk or paint the seats on German motorbikes (sometimes leaving the imprint on the trousers!), on roads, walls, houses and in the dust on the empty shop windows, anywhere – even on properties and pillars where Germans were living.

It was at this time that several V-signs in thick pencil was seen on German signposts around the Grandes Rocques area. The police constable who visited with the German police (Feldgendarmerie) felt that children were the culprits. I expect the children who were responsible were very nervous, as the Germans considered this act as sabotage. They, along with their parents and teachers had to attend the Castel school and were reprimanded by the Germans. I don't expect they continued their drawings after this!

The Germans eventually felt it best to join in and gave their V-sign too, but they always added the Laurel leaves underneath. There were V-signs everywhere around the Island with one still showing on a house in the Grange.

It was in 1942, a year or so after this campaign started that Roy Machon and Alf spoke by chance to a young Belgian. He showed them an English coin which he had worked on and chipped away, leaving the King's Head inside a V-sign. Both men decided they would try making the same but try to improve them and make them into a badge. Alf made them in the dairy of his dad's farm with a workshop close by and Roy, who worked as a projectionist at the Regal Cinema, would make them while the Germans watched films!

Alf and Roy would wear them on the inside label of their jackets so that passing Germans could not see their badges. They were made very well and news soon made the rounds. Soon trusted friends also wanted these special V badges and the men made between 300–400 for both men and women. The public would bring the coins, either pennies, sixpences, shillings, florins or half crowns and when finished, Alf and Roy would charge a Mark (Occupation Reichmark worth approximately 2 and a penny or 10p now) for making them.

They improved in the finishing of them and Alf continued until the end of the war. Unfortunately Roy was caught openly wearing one by the Germans and he was sentenced to six months in a camp in Munich. He spent one month in prison in Guernsey, then one day free before being taken to Munich. Roy wanted a party before leaving so hired a cafe and arranged a get-together with friends and had a good sing-song such as 'Hang out the washing' etc but unfortunately next door was the German Naval HQ and when leaving some of the friends, found the Germans with bayonets at the ready had surrounded the building. Some of the friends dashed back to take the V-signs and bunting etc down and to warn the others, but some forty to fifty of them were kept in prison overnight because they hadn't carried their identity cards. A month later they were interviewed again and warned if caught again, they would all be sent to Germany. Roy was sent to Munich for six months, then sent to an internment camp at Laufen until the end of the war. Afterwards, he returned to Guernsey.

Alf says he was certainly a dare-devil and quite a character and always felt he was the original one to start the V-signs around Guernsey.

Apparently, whilst working as the projectionist, Roy invited Alf around one evening to be with him. There would always be a newsreel with British and German troops in battle. At the films, there was a centre pole dividing the local population and the Germans. Roy instructed Alf to use a switch to turn up the volume very loud when the film showed the British troops firing but to put the sound down when the Germans opened up. I am sure 'they' were not amused but nothing came of it this time.

V-sign badges and brooches

Another crash landing Heinkel III (J. Priaulx)

German troops marching past the market and the town church

Bill Gillingham's Memoirs

Bill Gillingham is a popular Islander who has many interests and has a good sense of humour, hence he has many friends (including André and myself) on the Island. In his own words, he has written his account which I think is wonderful as he remembers so many finer details and work places from so long ago:

He begins, June 19th 1940. Announcement of Evacuation. First boats with women and children left on Friday morning June 21st.

My mother who was then aged 48, volunteered as a helper to go with children of Hautes Capelles School. There was no room on the boat the day they were due to go. When she returned the next day, quite a number of parents had changed their minds about letting their children go so her help was not needed. I was surprised to see her home when I arrived back from work for the second day as dad and I had decided to hang on a little longer. In fact, I had decided to remain here as only about two weeks earlier, I had had my first serious date with what I thought was the loveliest and most appealing girl in the Vale parish who I courted right through the Occupation and married on June 6th 1946. Leith Hubert became my soul mate and the best wife anyone could have for the next 53 years and four months. I doubt whether this would have happened had I evacuated. Therefore, I have never had many regrets at not having evacuated!

An amusing anecdote to the above was that dad had specified where (if we eventually all did evacuate), the keys to the back and front doors were to be hidden.

Thursday June 27th. A large German plane flew quite low over the Island. The next day, Friday June 28th at about 4pm, I was serving a customer at Le Riches Bridge Cash Stores (now the Guernsey Press Shop) when we heard a strange noise as well as the noise of planes. Someone came running into the shop and said the planes were German and that they were machine gunning all over the Island and that they had bombed the harbour.

The Managing Director of Le Riches, Mr H. Collings, had just arrived as was his usual weekly custom at about 2pm every Friday with our wage packets of around 30/- (£1.50). Just a few minutes before the air raid, he immediately ordered the shop to be closed and he joined all the staff in the cellar under the shop. We all remained therefore for about 20 minutes until the sound of aircraft had passed.

Bill reading his book to me

Mr Collings then asked Mr Bert Simon, the manager who lived over the shop, to remain on the premises in case anyone should need any urgent food, but told the remainder of staff to go home and hoped we would find our loved ones safe.

When I arrived home at Osmond House, Coutanchez, St Sampsons (the three storey house opposite the lane leading to Grow Limited) at approximately 5.30pm; mother said dad had gone off on his bike to answer an emergency call from the AFS (Auxiliary Fire Service) which he had joined soon after the outbreak of war in September 1939.

Dad returned home at about 11pm that night in quite a state, both physically and mentally as he had helped to put out the fire at the London Sheds which were set alight in the bombing (these are the first sheds on the right going down to the White Rock from the Weighbridge). Dad also witnessed some of the carnage caused to the lorries and their drivers waiting to unload their trays of tomatoes. Dad's uniform was in quite a mess as the London Sheds contained all kinds of goods which had recently arrived via the London boats. This included an amount of sulphur which dad said had almost choked some of the fire-fighters and which made quite a mess of their uniforms.

Saturday June 29th. I went to work where everyone was talking about the air raid. Pictures appeared in the local press and *Star*. When I arrived home at 6pm, both mum and dad were very upset as dad had phoned Doctor Foote, the vet to come and put down our dear dog, Rover, who was 12-years-old and was very distressed during the air raid. Not knowing what we were all going to do, Rover was beginning to have health problems and dad had thought it best to have him put down which was I am sure, a wise decision!

Sometime during the Saturday, aunt Mabel (mum's sister and Mrs Mont of Le Hamel Farm situated between Rue Mainguy and Pleinheaume) had phoned to say we should consider leaving home as it was too close to the gasworks which the Germans might attack so we (mum, dad and me) rode to Le Hamel Farm and slept there that Saturday and Sunday night.

*The gas mask that Bill's mother was to take with
her, still in excellent condition after 65 years*

On the Sunday morning (June 30th) I was in the yard at Le Hamel Farm when
we heard the sound of motorcycles and sure enough, two German motorcycles and
sidecars (driver, pillion passenger and also one in sidecar with rifle at the ready)
passed the farm and drove straight up to the mill, an old mill on high ground
which overlooked quite an area of the north west coast of the Islands (how did
they know their way there?)

OCCUPIED

From now on, we went about our daily lives as best we could. At Le Riches, we
tried to allocate what stocks we had as fairly as possible – one large tin of fruit to
a family of four or a half tin to a family of two, one tin of fish or meat per family
essentials such as sugar, butter, fats, tea etc were on official rationing.

Early in December of 1940, Mr Jim Guilbert of La Rochelle Farm stopped me
on the bridge one day and told me he intended opening a shop on the bridge to
sell local produce, fruit and vegetables, and would I be interested in working for
him to manage the shop as he would not have time to be in the shop full-time. He
offered me five shillings a week more money extra to whatever Le Riches were
paying me at the present (25p at present day money) which was quite a substantial
amount in those days! I had a word with the manager of Le Riches who told me to
go ahead if I wished, as he didn't know just how long the Occupation would last
and how long there would be enough food to warrant keeping on a full staff. So
I duly accepted Mr Jim Guilbert's offer and remained in his employment until the
spring of 1942.

Before going on to the selection procedures may I just make one or two remarks as to my time in charge of Jim's vegetable shop.

During the time working for Mr Guilbert, we were not allowed to sell any vegetables to any of the armed forces or the O.T., nor were we supposed to sell to any of the Foreign Forced Labourers, but we did occasionally supply some of the unfortunate forced labourers with a few parsnips or swedes and marrows. It was really pitiful to see these people, mostly Algerians, in the winter of 1941 coming into the shop with only wet sacking on their feet. Quite a number of them were housed in wooden huts which the Germans had built in a field below the Delancey cottages, the field which was on the right hand side of the road leading up from the Round Chimney.

I was one of some 200 men of military age to be called up by a letter and told to report at 9am on a certain day at Summerland House, Mount Durand (now a nursing home).

When I reported as ordered at Summerland House, I realised that I would be only one of many local 'boys' who would be forced to work for Mr Hitler. Among those present that morning I remember seeing Gordon Hough, mine host of the Mariners public house at the bridge, George Hurrel (who was to become my workmate until the end of the Occupation and who was a butcher for the Elliston Bros, in the meat market), Dick Smith, another butcher, Ted Thoume, a fellow grocer by trade and who worked for Luff and Co, family grocers, etc. When my name was called to be 'assessed', I entered quite a large room to be confronted by a table approximately five to six feet in length. Sitting in the centre was a man I recognised as Mr Isler, mine host of the Hotel de Normandie in Le Fevre Street/Berthelot Street, St Peter Port. On either side of him sat two German officers. I believe Mr Isler recognised me at once, as when I was the boy at Le Riches, High Street, there

St Sampson's School 'Occupied' (J. Priaulx)

were times when the Hotel de Normandie would find themselves short of bacon in the morning, and the chef would phone down for one or two pounds of back rashers urgently and yours truly would be sent up right away with the order. I saw Mr Isler on more than one occasion and always said 'Good Morning Sir' as was customary in those days. I believe this little act of politeness paid off as when Mr Isler looked at me, I'm sure he gave a faint smile. Consequently he must have advised the German Officers that I would be most suitable to work in the food store for which I was most grateful. Much better than sitting down oiling and greasing ammunition all day long!

We were made to sign a document which noted that if we stole any articles or damaged any installations belonging to the occupying Forces, it would be recognised as an act of sabotage for which the penalty could be deportation or death, so although we all did steal if and when the opportunity arose, I maintain we never broke the commandment 'Thou shall not steal', we were committing sabotage!

Although we were now in the period of the Occupation when the Black Market was rife (and prosperous for some!), I never ever sold any of the flour or whatever other foodstuff I had managed to 'borrow off the Fuhrer' because apart from mum, dad and myself, we had gran and grandpa Gillingham to think of. Also an elderly aunt and uncle who lived in St Martins plus my fiancée Leith and her parents so we did try and share it around. Only on two occasions towards the end of 1944 a farmer approached my mother and asked if she knew anyone that could exchange one pound of flour for a small piece of beef. So mother asked me if I would be willing to make a swap so I agreed – this happened just twice about a month to six months apart.

Sabotage or Pilfering?
There were ways and means!

I will now try and give an account of what work we were told to do for the Verpflegungsacis Gahestelle, Guernsey (which I believe briefly translated meant 'the German Army Food Stores' under the command of Oberzahlmeister, Langer).

Flour was imported in good quality 75 kilo sacks. We would have to unload them from either lorries or horse driven German wagons and take them on our backs up approximately 16 stairs at Youngs Stores (now I believe Goulds Carters Store). This was the most dreaded store as all the others such as Vale church hall, Salvation Army hall – L'Islet, Ker Maria and Vauvert Schools, St Andrews Arsenal and Baubigny Arsenal were all on the flat. Once the cargo was in the stores, all the bags had to be stacked, two standing, one across and another two on top and every three weeks, these stacks had to be knocked down, the top rolled and then restacked. This was to prevent the flour from 'going mileg'. It was during this latter operation that when the German guard was not looking, we would loosen the tied neck of the sack so that when it fell to the floor, some flour would spill out which was when we would manage to take two or three handfuls in our little canvas bags which we always carried. Provided we did not overdo it, the German guards were always willing to turn a blind eye. They knew we were short of food.

Also with only one exception, all the German guards were over 40 and were not of the 'Nazi breed'. All they wanted was for the war to finish to get back to their wives.

One German guard named Willy Kirch, a tubby 5'3" or 5'4" who would always say 'Krieg ist chiser' (war is ———. I will leave you, the reader, to do your own translation of this last word). About three years after 2001, I was talking to a local business man, now deceased, from the north of the Island about the occupation and it transpired this man became quite friendly with Willy Kirch as apparently Willy did not like the German bread so whenever he was on guard at the Salvation Army hall, L'Islet, he would arrange for this man to go along after midnight and collect about 30–40lbs of flour for his mother to bake him some bread. Apparently Willy would untie maybe 8 or 10 bags of flour and take a few pounds out of each and then re-tie them. This local man lived quite close to the old L'Islet Salvation Army hall and Willy knew all the guard's movements.

Potatoes – cargos of potatoes arrived from France, not in sacks but loose in the hold of one of the small cargo ships which plied mainly between either St Malo or Grouville. I am not sure how they were taken out of the hold but local lorries with local drivers would come up St Julian's Avenue and down Le Truchot as far as the entrance to the two tunnels situated opposite what was Strangers Mineral Water Factory now a bank complex. These tunnels were approximately 130' to 150' long. Once the tail board of the lorry was let down, some potatoes would fall on to the road and roll down under the lorry. We always made sure enough potatoes fell off the lorry to supply one or two elderly women who lived nearby, also a few children who soon found themselves there. The potatoes were forked into the large wicker baskets which were used to unload coal from the coal boats before the war. These baskets held over one hundredweight of potatoes and we had to carry them down three or four steps to the tunnel entrance then along the length of the tunnels. The distance obviously got shorter as the tunnel gradually filled. We worked in groups of six carrying for half-hour periods then changing to filling up the baskets or lifting the baskets from the road onto the back of the person who's turn it was to carry! The German guard in charge of this operation was nicknamed 'Booter'. He was an ex-boxer who had suffered a broken nose. He also sported a cauliflower ear – not the most handsome of Germans. His nickname derived from the fact that if he didn't think we were working fast enough, he would come behind us and boot us up the backside – never really hard. He would then turn around and give a grin. He would sometimes pretend to go towards the old ladies who occasionally would reach over the side of the lorries to try and grab a few extra potatoes and show them his boot. Children would also be chased away if there were too many of them around. All except one – a lovely cheeky blonde curly haired little girl of about four or five years of age. She could get away with anything. We found out her name was Molly and lived in Les Canichers with her parents. She grew up into a smashing teenager and married a chap by the name of Bihet!

I must say here that at the end of the day, Booter would always allow us to take home what he would say three kilos, but we usually managed to come away with nearer to 10 pounds.

One rather frightening experience which six of us had was one morning we were sent to a tunnel lower down Le Truchot. It was a tunnel in which the post office used to garage their vans and was just a few yards above the rear entrance to the Gaumont Cinema, right opposite of what is today the underground car park of Wheadon House. We were standing at the tunnel entrance waiting for the first lorry load to arrive when we heard a plane flying fairly low. Suddenly, we were almost knocked over flat on to our backs. What had happened was the previous day one of our planes had flown over the town area and spotted a German submarine moored in the old harbour right in front of the Woolworths/Creasey shops. Quite rightly, the 'powers that be' decided to drop a stick of bombs as near as possible to it the following morning. It was the blast from these bombs which almost knocked us over and which also smashed almost every shop window in the High Street and the Pollet. All to no avail as the Germans realised that the British reconaissance plane the previous day would have spotted their submarine moored in the harbour so during the night, they moved it and moored it in Fermain Bay!

The most frightening thing which happened to the six of us boys was that the German guard in charge of us made us follow him into a German air raid shelter deep below what was the White Hart public house (now a night club) as the Germans had built a strong gun position right on the corner of the bottom of the Pollet. This position covered the whole of the Weighbridge area. To be entombed in this concrete chamber 10 or 12 feet underground was, for me, one of the most frightful experiences of the whole of the Occupation.

Hay and straw – bales of to supply the needs of the horse population which the Germans had brought over to supplement their motor/lorry transport, was another fairly strenuous job which we had to do, stacking those bales 12 to 15 high. The two main locations for storing was in the road directly behind St George's Hall. Along the road which led from Piette Road to Paris Street, was an open area where these bales were stacked. The other area was in Mont Arrive, an area which had been occupied by W. Head and Sons, General Carters etc where now there is a fitness centre and a second-hand clothing complex.

Unlike having to work unloading the 'spud cart', no one liked having to unload bales of hay and straw. 'No perks here!' We had not been reduced to eating hay yet!

Having been chosen to work in the food stores, I was told to report at 8am the next morning at the German food store HQ which were the sheds behind the now Absolute End restaurant. Before the war, these sheds were where agents exported tomatoes and flowers.

This HQ was known as Le Boullion Stores which remained our HQ until some time in 1944 when, following the air raid on the submarine in the town harbour, the HQ was moved to what was Melrose School for Girls in Rosaire Avenue.

But let's begin at the Boullion HQ where every morning at 8am sharp, the 25 or so of us would line up in front of the stores. On the Monday morning, seven of us (the same seven every Monday) would be detailed to accompany one of the German soldiers to go to one of the depots to collect the bulk rations for distribution the next day. Tuesday was the day the various German units came from all over the Island, mainly with horse-drawn wagons but with lorries from the further afield units. The seven of us were each given a specific commodity to issue against a special voucher which Raymond, the German officer in charge of issuing the vouchers, would give us. One week maybe I would be issuing rice so I would be given a voucher for maybe two kilos of rice. The next week I might be given the job of issuing beans or perhaps another week, it could be salt etc, etc. Whatever we were given to issue, we would always try and put two or three handfuls in our pockets in the morning and again in the afternoon. Raymond spoke very good English. He told us he had been to a university in England to learn English to teach in a German school. He was another German who turned a blind eye to our sabotage providing we did not overdo it.

One amusing incident happened when I was given the job of issuing salted herrings. Five barrels full had arrived about six months after the Germans had captured Norway, so when I arrived home for dinner at 12.30pm, mother would always ask on Tuesdays 'What are you on today Bill?' So this day I said 'Salted herrings', and 'I want a pair of dad's long johns' (long underpants). 'Whatever for?' she asked. I said that I would put on the long johns first, then my ordinary trousers and lastly the blue trousers which the Germans had issued to us (they also issued us with a blue jacket with a red flash on the collar so that we could be identified). So it was when I arrived home from work that afternoon at approximately 6pm, when I got off my bike and walked the six or eight steps towards the back door, I was greeted by our two cats meowing around me. I had four herrings down each trouser leg between my trousers and dad's long johns (the cats did have the fish heads)!

THE RED CROSS

Moving to Melrose School proved fairly uneventful but it was during this period that the Island was getting very short of food. Even the German troop rations were being reduced and so it was one of the most eventful days that Guernsey is ever likely to record when the Red Cross ship *Vega* arrived on December 27th 1944 although towards the end of 1944, the Germans did tend to turn a blind eye to our little acts of sabotage (pilfering). The time had now arrived when they were being short-rationed and they became really tough on anyone they saw pilfering so we were all most grateful for the Red Cross parcels. Going to bed and having difficulty in sleeping due to feeling hungry is not a pleasant sensation!

It was always an exciting experience going to collect our Red Cross parcels whether it was a Canadian or a New Zealand parcel. After we had consumed the tinned powdered milk, I took the empty tin to Bougourd and Harry, Vale Avenue, who soldered on a tin handle for one or two marks which gave Mother an extra small saucepan. I also remember when the *Vega* brought some lovely pure white flour. We ate the bread made from this flour as if it was cake! Prior to the arrival of the *Vega*, the Red Cross messages from our loved ones in England were so very much appreciated!

CRYSTAL SET

One thing which I think kept us going was the fact that I had a crystal set right through the Occupation, which meant that I heard the BBC overseas news daily and hearing about the progress that our troops were making certainly helped us to hope that Liberation would not be too far away. When Liberation Day did arrive, my parents and I were invited to the caretaker's top flat at the States Offices (now the Tourist Office). Mr Cliff Bichard and his wife had been tenants of the Wing at Osmond Lane before and for a few months into the Occupation until offered the job as caretaker of the States Offices. The five of us were in their lounge on the top floor of the States Office when Cliff Bichard, who had kept a small wireless, turned it on to hear Sir Winston Churchill give his famous speech namely:

'At three o'clock this afternoon, our dear Channel Islands will be freed.' I can say without shame or hesitation that there was not a dry eye in that room!

The crystal set which meant a great deal to Bill

Further Aspects of Guernsey
by Helmut Methner

André and I can hardly believe we have lived in Rose-Adele, a six roomed bungalow, for almost three years. It is literally just down the road from Woodcote, Les Canichers, our home for many years and having so many memories, together with Rose Villa, situated almost opposite and where I was born and also my sister, mother and all the Collins family from way back.

Finally, after 39 years of catering and holiday self-catering, we decided to change house so that we could relax a little but still wanting a garden – especially André – as this has always been his work and he was still enjoying outside hobbies. I still miss the wonderful sea views we had at Woodcote, especially looking out early morning and seeing the sun rising over Herm and Sark. Many were really spectacular, hence the dozens of photographs I have taken!

Now, we very much enjoy the dozens of wild birds that feed daily in the garden and are amazed how many visit us considering we live just out of the town.

HELMET METHNER

There is another little story to tell you regarding Woodcote. It would be difficult for me to have a guess as to how many people have stayed and passed through the doors there. Besides the full rooms used throughout the summer seasons when we enjoyed meeting new and old friends for those many years, there was also the many forced foreign workers who lived there during the Occupation. Now we have found out just by chance that German sailors also lived there for some time. Before I start to tell you how this all came about, you will notice that our home now is called Rose-Adele (we changed it from Toowoomba!). Woodcote was originally called Rose-Adele years ago! The previous owners changed the name to Woodcote from Rose-Adele but you may have realised, we do like the house name, hence the bungalow change. My early years were in Rose Villa and then Mon Reve (my dream). We then moved to a house called Rosedale so it just had to be another Rose!

It was on 2nd July 1999 (date given by letter as you will see) that André, and I arrived home at Woodcote to find our daughter, Carol, talking to an elderly gentleman and a younger lady at our gate. They had been looking for a house called Rose-Adele and it emerged that they were a German father and daughter, Helmut P. Methner and Brigitte Methner-Opel. This intrigued us and of course we invited them indoors and were very interested to meet them and hear what they had to say. As promised, they wrote and sent photographs (printed) when they returned and although Helmut spoke little English, Brigitte spoke and wrote good English, so it seemed Helmut wrote his memoirs and Brigitte translated and typed this letter to us which is printed here, word for word:

My Aspects Of Guernsey
by Helmut P. Methner

Besides the Germans you describe in your books, the Todt's (we called 'OT' which meant Organisation Todt) and those special POWs, the 'slave workers' as you call them, there was a division of the German navy for the harbour defence. The administration office was at 'Glategny Esplanade' around Wyndhams Hotel as it is called today (now Marina Court) and the night club next door, opposite the new Queen Elizabeth II Marina.

In 1942 the marina did not exist. Behind the pier shelter there was nothing but the open sea. I remember, when there was stormy weather and heavy seas the surf crashed against the windowpanes of our office. In August 1942, after having accomplished my education as a boat's mate, I was ordered to Guernsey to get the command of my own boat. I just had 18 years and 8 months. Already two years ago in 1940 the army had called me, not yet 17 years old, because I had signed in as a volunteer for the navy, to avoid having to join the Armed Forces as a normal soldier.

At the Guernsey Harbour Fleet I got the command for a boat which had been a trawler before. Later on my ship was a former custom cruiser. Besides the bunks for the 10 to 12 men there was a little galley on the boat to cook meals for the crew. Our armament was an anti-aircraft gun, some machine guns and some other small guns. Fortunately during my time in Guernsey none of them has every been used.

It was one of my duties to bring couriers for the other troops being stationed in Guernsey to the mainland of France such as St. Malo or Granville and to the other Channel Islands like Jersey, Alderney or Sark. The poor communication technology at this time required a personal courier service. Today after I had taken the opportunity to visit the touristic attractions of the Channel Islands, Guernsey and Jersey, I begin to realise how naive and lucky I was as a young inexperienced guy to ship around with my little boat between cliffs and underwater rocks without ever being in distress. This has to be regarded under the aspects that around St. Malo Bay and the Channel Islands is a maximum tides' difference of 14m and a current up to 8 or 10 nautical miles. For such a critical area my boat was only primitively equipped. We were able to morse and had a magnet compass on board. The maximum speed of my boat was between 7 and 8 nautic miles/hour, which was exactly the speed of the normal current.

Watching this current carefully was the highest priority in my job. But the 'bogy-man', the invisible patron of all seamen, was always with me and protected me and my crew all this time.

When I came to Guernsey for the first time, I did not know much about the history of the Occupation. The history of the Island was completely unknown by us. (And to be honest, we were not really interested in knowing better either). In our eyes Guernsey was above everything else the place where wealthy British pensioners or honourable Colonial officers were enjoying their retirement. That everything was a bit poorer than at the French mainland – I had been based in Cherbourg before – was easily to be seen. There nearly were no shops to buy something. Restaurants practically did not exist. The lack of food has been explained to us through bad weather and the therefore missing transport vessels. Under those conditions I also had been playing a 'potato game.'

Once in a day we heard: potatoes are getting short. As we did not have a fix berth for our boat at the harbour, we used to go alongside with the freight ships, unloading their freight at the pier. We found the shop loaded with potatoes to the top and went alongside. The unloading had been organised by the Todt and their POWs. We realised that the Todts were very rude to the Russians who did not have the slightest chance to catch only one of the potatoes for themselves. So we found a way to make them get what they needed. For the Todts it was impossible to watch the Russians all the time though. So while unloading the potatoes some of the bags fell by chance or by accident on my boat's deck. One of them disappeared immediately under deck for my own crew. For the Russians, who were not completely unguilty concerning this accident, we cooked a huge pot of potatoes, from which they could eat themselves fill, one after the other, hidden before the eyes of the Todts under deck.

Games like that, being dangerous for us Marine guys, became our favourite play. We were young and fearless and it turned out right all the time. Very soon, we realised that the other soldiers on the Island were not so well equipped with food as the navy was. The navy is always something special. When couriers came on board, we regularly cooked a big pot of soup. Every Landser as we called them, got his cup of soup and a piece of bread. With us in the navy, food was always plentiful.

With the people of Guernsey we did not have many relations, but no problems either. Someday we got to know a young girl – (the daughter Brigette's comment – this girl was clever enough to be nice to all the young seamen without preferring any special one of them, keeping them all at a friendly distance, so that she never got in trouble by their jealousy) and some other young civilians joined her. We also met her grandmother who got black tea and sugar from us.

Now I want to talk about Rose-Adele, the house called Woodcote today, which is the link in the chain that ties our two stories together.

The time I was not on duty when the ship was at the harbour, I did not have to sleep on board. For these days we were allowed to stay in a private house close to the harbour. This house was Rose-Adele, Les Canichers 35. I used to live there with five other boatswains of our fleet. In our time – August 42 until spring 43 – there were no Todt POWs in Rose-Adele. The owners of this house we did not get to know. The name of the street slipped out of my memory very quickly. But Rose-Adele became our second home in Guernsey! And together with that a symbol for a small piece of normal life in these terrible times, the reason why its picture was burnt so deeply into the soul of my father and had to be found again.

Helmut Methner with seamen outside Rose-Adele

Outside Dowding's shop

And this is how I came to the story; 'How I recovered Rose-Adele'. For my 70th birthday, my daughter had the idea of a 'travel into the past' as a present for my wife and me. For Easter 1994 she booked a trip to the Island of Jersey using the ferry from St. Malo and with the option of another ferry from Jersey to Guernsey, where I had been when I was a young navy soldier at St. Peter Port for three quarters of a year. In a souvenir box we found some old photographs showing me and my fellow boatswains in front of Rose-Adele and in front of the Dowding shop on the opposite side of the street. With those photos I hoped to find Rose-Adele again. Unfortunately in this time of the year – how it might often be in this area – it was the bad weather that made it impossible for my daughter, who joined us together with her family for this week in Jersey, and me to come to Guernsey. During the whole week there were no boats to go because of the heavy sea. It was a shame! We had to go back to St. Malo (with the big car ferry, which could go even in heavy weather). Rose-Adele still remained nothing but a memory.

But it would not have been my daughter Brigitte, resting contented with this situation. The next important date in our family was 25th May 1999. This was the day when my wife Mia and I had been happily married for 50 years. To say it in German, we celebrated our 'Goldene Hochzeit.' This was a good date for Brigitte. She organised for us (including our son-in-law Claus and our grandson Tobias as it has been before) a journey to the Normandy with (again) the option of a ferry trip from Dielette to Guernsey. This time we had chosen a (weatherwise) much 'safer' season, the summer in June/July. So Brigitte and I could go on board of the ferry to Guernsey on July 2nd 1999 at 7.30 a.m. – my wife Mia had suffered an accident with her foot and besides that has a little fear of the big sea. That's the reason why I only made this trip together with my daughter, even if I would have liked to show my wife a little piece of my past.

This past came up to me when we entered the harbour of St. Peter Port, certainly we had my two famous photos in the pocket. Even if the harbour did change a lot, I could recognise the most places, because the pier and Castle Cornet still stood at the same place as they did in 1942. But how to find Rose-Adele? First we met two elderly men fishing at the pier. We showed the photos and told a bit about my special story. One of them thought he would recognise the street, but as he was not sure he told us to go to the Tourist Office, where they might help us. People there were very kind to us looked at the photos, listened to our story, but could not provide any assistance. They were too young and could not remember the time 57 years ago, But they had the idea that we should go to the Guernsey Museum, where the history of Guernsey is being preserved and somebody might have the right age to remember the Occupation time. We made our way to the museum. Same procedure becoming a routine in between: questions, photos, story. The man at the information desk was friendly and seemed to be interested, but the lady that might have helped us unfortunately was not available this day. But he gave us the hint to go and see the old library. To us it was evident that this would be the last chance and we did not hesitate to take this. And off we went to the library. We found a gentleman at his desk who took an extremely polite interest in our story. He examined the photos carefully. Then suddenly, when he watched the one showing the opposite side of Rose-Adele and recognised

'Dowding' and 'Bichard', we had the impression of a slight flickering light in his eyes. He once again stated the date of the photographs then he resolutely took a small red book out of one shelf – the telephone book of Guernsey 1942. Then it only took a short glimpse and we got to know that the address of Rose-Adele was Les Canichers 35. As a sign of thankfulness, we left the old photographs with the friendly gentleman at the Library. He was proud he could show us some old journals in his archive. This time a Guernsey Zeitung written in German had been published, that we sailors did not know about. Then we happily left the library to our final expedition. First time we went down the street Les Canichers we passed the house by without remarking it. As we did not watch the house numbers and as I had a fairly grey house in mind not a freshly painted one as it was now, I did not recognise it at once. On the second try we did watch the numbers and found the windows which must have been the shop windows of Dowdings. So I went to the opposite side of the street. This must be our house, but it was not named Rose-Adele it was called Woodcote.

Dear Mrs Molly, the continuation of the story you did experience and influence by yourself. Let me take this opportunity to thank you again for the gift of the two books *A Child's War* and *Reflections of Guernsey*. I have read most of it and I have learned a lot out of them, I did not know when I was a young sailor in Guernsey in 1942. We are still so grateful and happy how luckily everything turned out for us and we definitely will live on that for a very long time. Maybe it was the same bogy-man, I had on board this long time ago, who helped me this time again – at least a little bit.

Myself and Helmut at Woodcote

Guernsey Occupation Recipes

Many Occupation recipes were printed in the *Star* newspaper during these years, all to help out the meagre rations and when fruit and vegetables were in season, you might find some of interest.

SAME ROOTS, DIFFERENT FRUITS

1945, Dr A. N. Symons, Guernsey's medical services officer, wrote the following to help the Islanders:

It is known that where there has been severe shortage, the decline in health of the population is gradual until the end which eventually comes suddenly. It has been compared to a vehicle going down an inclined plain and then suddenly over a precipice.

Were it not for the untiring efforts of the Channel Islands' Kitchen Front, it is quite possible that the civilian population might have succumbed before the arrival of the freighter, *Vega* ; and her cargo of food parcels.

At the end of the Occupation, it was noted that the food situation was actually worse for the Germans than for the civilians. A number of Germans suffered from malnutrition and anaemia and were emaciated.

The following recipes have been selected from many created by a beleaguered population during five years of almost unbelievable hardship. Most of these wartime recipes can be made today. Most are highly nutritious and cheap to make.

Imitation Suet Pudding

Ingredients:
8oz flour
Small teaspoon salt
4oz raw, peeled potatoes
Cold water to mix

Put the flour and salt into a basin, grate the potatoes and mix with the flour and sufficient water to form a soft dough. Put into a greased basin and steam for two hours.

Wartime Yorkshire Pudding

Ingredients:
4oz flour
½ pint buttermilk or sour milk
Pinch of salt
¼ teaspoon bicarbonate of soda
(Fresh milk and self-raising flour may be used; if so, omit the soda)

Sift the flour and salt into a basin and stir in the buttermilk. Beat well and stand aside for at least ½ hour. Mix the soda with a very little water or fresh milk and stir in just before cooking the batter.

Tomato Bread Spread

Dr A. N. Symons continues :

Many of us regret that we are unable to use as many tomatoes as we would like, owing, as working class people, to not being able to stock sugar and salt. When my wife was here, we always had tomato chutney and tomato sauce made each season. Before giving you a useful recipe, I wish to state that I have given some of the undermentioned to several of my friends to sample and they liked it. Before the war, I had this spread on bread and butter but under war conditions, this will be quite good on bread alone, having margarine included.

Ingredients:
½ lb tomatoes
1oz margarine
1oz grated cheese
1 egg
Salt and pepper

Skin and pulp the tomatoes, add the margarine and cook for a few minutes. Add the cheese, seasoning and the beaten egg. Stir gently but do not boil. When thick, pour into small jars and cover when cold.

I generally allow the pulp of an extra tomato to allow for any hard centres in the ½ pound, which it is advisable to extract when pulping.

PARSNIP PUDDING

Ingredients:
Cooked, cold parsnip
Cocoa substitute
Bicarbonate of soda
½ pint warm milk
Sugar or sweetener

Mix all the ingredients together and place in a greased pie-dish. Bake for ½ hour.

BREAD AND CHEESE CUSTARD

Ingredients:
Bread and butter
1 cupful grated cheese
1 pint milk
2 eggs
Pepper and salt

Grease a pie-dish, cover the bottom with bread and butter, cover with grated cheese, then bread and butter again and more cheese. The last layer should have butter on top. Beat the eggs; add the milk, salt and pepper. Pour into the dish and leave to soak for ½ hour. Cover with grated cheese and bake in a moderate oven for about ½ hour and serve hot.

DAMPER

(This recipe was published in the newspaper following several queries from readers as to its origin. The paper replied: 'As we remember it, it is a sort of bread made by bushmen in Australia, is quickly made and is very palatable.' Damper was apparently eaten in the Channel Islands at the turn of the century and revived during the Occupation).

Ingredients:
½lb self-raising flour
Large pinch salt
Enough water to mix a dry dough

POTATO PUDDING

Ingredients:
1lb potatoes
1oz sugar
1 or 2oz fruit
1 egg

Scrub the potatoes, but do not peel them. Beat the egg in a large basin and into this, grate finely the unpeeled potatoes, mixing frequently with the egg to prevent the potato becoming discoloured. Add the sugar and fruit and put in a well-greased pie-dish. Bake in a fairly hot oven for about one hour; or the pudding may be steamed for two hours. The fruit may be omitted and the pudding served with stewed fruit or a sweet sauce.

POTATO PEEL CAKE

Ingredients:
Several potatoes
4–5 tablespoons of flour
Sugar or sweetener to taste
1 teaspoon bicarbonate of soda
(or baking powder)
A little milk, pinch of salt
Flavouring if required

Scrub the potatoes and then peel them. Boil the peels only till soft, drain and mash or mince. Mix the flour with the peel and sweeten to taste. Add the bicarbonate of soda and salt and mix the whole with a little milk and flavour. Bake as for a cake. If preferred, instead of sugar, put onions and herbs and make a savoury cake. A few slices of tomato will improve the flavour. It can be boiled or steamed instead of baked.

POTATO SANDWICH

Ingredients:
¾–1lb of potatoes
1oz of butter
2oz of sugar
1 egg
A little milk

Cream the egg yolk, butter and sugar. Add the cooked potatoes, whipped to a cream with the milk. Add the white of egg and beat to a froth. Put into two greased sandwich tins and bake for half an hour.

BEAN AND POTATO CAKE

Simply make rissoles from equal quantities of mashed beans and mashed potatoes and fry them in very little fat.

POTATO TART

Ingredients:
Potato pastry
Potatoes
Sugar
Spice

Make some potato pastry and roll it out into two rounds. Cover one round with slices of raw potato the size of a five shilling piece. Over each layer, sprinkle a little sugar and cinnamon or other spice. Cover with the other round of pastry and pinch the sides well together. Bake slowly for an hour, take off the top and put in a few spoonfuls of custard or white sauce (cream in other days). Leave till cold and heat it up again when required.

SWEETCORN AND POTATO PIE

Ingredients:
1lb potatoes
1 small tin sweetcorn (if available)
1 onion
½ cup milk
2 tablespoons stale breadcrumbs
¼ oz margarine
Flour
Salt and pepper

Peel the potatoes thinly and cut them into slices. Half fill a pie-dish with them. Next put in the contents (drained) of a tin of sweetcorn and cover with the onion cut into thin slices. Put another layer of sliced potatoes on top, dredge with flour and sprinkle with salt and pepper. Pour in the milk and cover the dish with the breadcrumbs. Dot with margarine and bake for two hours.

SWEETCORN PUDDING

Simply mince sweetcorn, put it into a pie-dish, cover with milk, add sweetener to taste and bake in the oven till done.

Country Batter Pie

Braise some chopped vegetables (whatever available) in a little pork fat till tender. Put into a hot, greased pie-dish with slices of cooked sausage or other meat. Pour some batter over and bake in a hot oven for about half an hour.

Limpet Omelette

Ingredients:
2 quarts limpets
1 bay leaf
2 small leeks
1 egg
Parsley
Salt and pepper

Put the limpets into cold water, bring to the boil, strain and remove shells. Return limpets to the pan and simmer until quite tender with the bay leaf and a little pepper and salt. Strain. Remove the heads and strings of the limpets and mince the limpets. Chop the leeks and mix them with the limpets, adding parsley. Put a little fat into a frying pan, add the well-beaten egg and then add the limpet and leek mixture and fry till brown.

Stewed Ormers

Soak the ormers in salt water for ½ hour, then scrub them with a hard bristle brush. Put into clean water and wash until white. Take them out and beat them with a wooden rolling pin on a wooden chopping board until they become tender, but take care not to break them. Then brown the ormers in a frying pan with butter. They will then look like steak. Next put them in a stew pan with a large onion cut up, season with herbs to taste and cover with a thick gravy stock for eight hours. They should be as tender as veal cutlets but far more delicious!

(Courtesy of Rocquaine Live Shellfish Ponds, Guernsey)

Carrageen Relish

Boil apples or other available fruit and sweeten to taste. Cook carrageen as usual with milk and flavouring; mix all together and allow to set like a mould.

Tomato Pie

Ingredients:
Tomatoes
Butter
1 onion
Seasoning
Breadcrumbs

Butter a baking dish and cover the bottom with sliced tomato, dot with butter and season. Onto this, place a layer of fried onions. Repeat these layers until the dish is full, finishing with breadcrumbs. Bake for 20 minutes in a moderate oven.

Tomato Jam

Ingredients:
To every 1½ lbs of not too ripe tomatoes, add
½lb sugar
¼ oz carrageen
1 cup water

Pour boiling water over the tomatoes and leave for a few minutes. Then peel and slice the tomato and place in a saucepan with a cup of cold water, add a tablespoonful of sugar and the carrageen (previously soaked) and boil for 15 minutes. The jam is then ready to be placed in jars.

Carrot Pudding

Ingredients:
3oz breadcrumbs
1oz sugar
1oz margarine
1¼ pint milk
2 eggs
2 medium carrots
1 teaspoon ground ginger

Put the breadcrumbs, butter and sugar into a basin and pour the boiling milk over them. Clean and grate the carrots and add them, together with egg yolks and ginger to the soaked breadcrumbs. Stir in the stiffly beaten whites of egg and bake in a moderate oven till firm and well browned. Serve with custard or ginger sauce.

Turnip Jam

Ingredients:
1 ½lbs turnips
1 ½ pints of water
1 teaspoon flavoured xarrageen
(Carre's Powdered Carravita)
1 cupful of raspberry cordial

Boil the turnips until tender, then mince them. Put back into water, add the raspberry cordial and carrageen and boil for five minutes. Allow to cool and pour into jars and cover.

Parsnips could also be made into jam, using orange juice as an alternative flavouring.

Guernsey Bean Jar/Jersey Bean Crock

This recipe is said to have been the inspiration behind baked beans. The traditional Channel Islands' Bean Jar, or Crock, is a centuries-old recipe which has many variations. In Jersey, the Bean Crock was served as a supper dish, while in Guernsey, the locals preferred to eat their Bean Jar for breakfast. In spite of food restrictions both Islands managed to preserve rudiments of the Bean Jar/Crock throughout the Occupation.

Put a nice meaty bone in a casserole with a few onions, carrots, a turnip and a pint of beans socked overnight in cold water Cover with plenty of water and season well. A teaspoonful of treacle and half a teaspoonful of mustard may be added. Almost any meat or vegetables will do and to save gas, a layer of potatoes can be put over the top.

Vegetarian Savoury Sausage

Ingredients:
½lb haricot beans
6lbs mashed potatoes
½lb onions
½lb tomatoes
2 oz margarine
4 teaspoons chopped parsley

Soak and cook the beans; fry the onions and tomatoes in the fat. Pass the beans and other ingredients through the mincer, mix well and add seasoning. Scale at 4oz, roll into sausages, dip in batter and fry a golden brown. These may also be made into balls, rolled in flour and baked in the oven.

Bean Flour

Using scarlet runner beans, dry the beans in the pod in a slow oven, pass them through a mincer, sift and return to the mincer until the whole has been converted into flour.

Bean Flour Cake

Ingredients:
½lb bean flour
3 oz fat
A little milk
1 oz sugar
Pinch of salt
A few sultanas

Rub the fat into the flour, mix the other ingredients with the milk; mix all together, put into a tin and bake in a moderate oven.

Parsnip Honey

Peel and wash 3lbs of parsnips. Cut into chunks and cover with cold water. Boil up sharply and simmer until soft. Drain off water but do not throw away. Mash the parsnips. Put liquid back into pan and add the mashed parsnips. Boil slowly and stir for 10 minutes. Pass the contents through a sieve. To each pound of puree add 4 oz of sugar; 1 teaspoonful of salt; 1 teaspoonful of ground ginger. Boil all together for eight minutes. Put into jars whilst hot.

As an alternative to ground ginger, crush a few cloves, tie in a muslin bag and boil with the parsnips. Remove the muslin bag when bottling.

Macaroni Cake

Ingredients:
2 oz macaroni, soaked and drained
2 oz flour
A little butter and milk
Baking powder

Mix the flour with the macaroni into a stiff mixture with the other ingredients. Bake for 20 minutes in a hot oven.

- Carrageen moss was an edible seaweed, collected when allowed on the beaches. Mainly sold (as collected) in the fish markets and was a setting and gelling agent, mainly used for puddings.

- Carre's Powdered Carravita – The Carrageen moss was dried and powdered by Carre's, a bakery and cake shop in the Arcade (town) and sold in small quantities.

- Limpets – a conical shell covering, the fish which strongly clings to the rocks.

- Ormer – (also called a sea-ear) an edible mollusc that has an ear shaped shell with holes, which also clings to rocks (breeds near the Channel Islands)

My thanks to Margaret for supplying the recipes printed above.

It was amazing how one managed to make a different dish with what was available at the time and to make the most of the limited rations we had, like fats and sugar. Eggs too were a luxury – very few recipes I have in the 'recipe' booklet mention eggs.

One can imagine the joy of Mrs Sims who years before had been a professional cook and was now looking forward to the Red Cross food parcels promised to arrive soon. This cake card was made by the well-known Guernsey artist, Bert Hill – a printer also working for the *Star* newspaper. He made it for Mr Irvin and Mrs Madeleine Sims (who kindly loaned it to me) to send to Mr Irvin's mother who had also been a professional cook years before. I just wonder what her thoughts were at the time!

Birthday Greetings
November 6th
1944

To dear Mum
From Irvin & Madeleine
With much love

PART TWO

Guernsey News in Britain Soon After the Evacuation

The separation and the lack of information from evacuees who left in June 1940, not knowing where children were staying, how they were and who were they with must have been dreadful. Many I am sure worried how they would fare on a sea journey, the majority never having set foot on a boat before. Husbands in the forces and with wives left behind, were they in the thick of the war? Were the Germans treating their loved ones well? Families were separated and just waiting for some news but many months went by before news came through.

Mr A.J. Sherwill helped to relieve these fears by recording a transmission by wireless from Guernsey with information particularly for Guernsey evacuees. Message as follows dated August 1940:

Gratefully, Victor Carey, the Governor and Bailiff of Guernsey accepted the offer of sending a message from 'the Island of Guernsey' (by the German Commandant) for transmission over the German radio reassuring to those separated that the German Occupation took place without a single person being harmed and that although not happy being occupied, we were being treated with courtesy and consideration. Signed and dated July 6th 1940.

'This is His Majesty's Procureur in Guernsey, Channel Islands, speaking to the people of the United Kingdom and in particular to those who left Guernsey and Alderney during the Evacuation which preceded the Guernsey ones. I imagine that many of you must be greatly worried as to how we are getting on. Well, let me tell you. Some will fear that I am making this record with a revolver in my head by a German Officer. The actual case is very different.

The Lieutenant Governor and Bailiff, Mr Victor Carey and every other Island official has been and is being treated with every consideration and with the greatest of courtesy by the German Military Authorities. The Island Government is functioning, churches and chapels are open for public worship. Banks, shops and places of entertainment are open as usual. Naturally, the sudden and entire severance of communications with the UK created innumerable problems with which we have wrestled and are still wrestling. Perhaps the best indications of the measure of our success will be shown by the latest figures of unemployment which are as follows:

Males unemployed (of which hardly any are fit for manual labour) 186, females unemployed 191. Relief by way of public assistance is not above the normal figures.'

Mr A.J. Sherwill continues to thank the controlling committee which has been set up to speed up public business, who have worked like Trojans.

He continues 'We have been occupied for four and a half weeks' and states he and the committee will stay intensely loyal subjects of His Majesty and this has been made clear to the German Commandant and his staff.

On a personal note, he sent good wishes and love to teachers and scholars of all schools evacuated and to all men of military age who left to join His Majesty's Forces 'God Speed' and to all wives, mothers and sweethearts 'God's Blessing.' To all Guernsey children his message was 'God keep you safe' and to all 'God Bless you till we meet again.' Mr A.J. Sherwill finishes 'Will the BBC please re-transmit this message and will the daily papers use it.'

These messages must have brought much comfort at that time and was signed and dated August 1940 (as printed in a *Channel Island Monthly Review*).

LIFE IN OCCUPIED TERRITORY
by Dr Casper

How the Guernsey people were facing a grim struggle to live was described by a member of the German Forces whilst in occupation of the Channel Islands and who subsequently became a prisoner of war in England.

'Residents in Guernsey have been stripped down to the bare essentials of existence. Everything is rationed – food, fuel and clothing. People have been evicted from their houses by the soldiers, others have been billeted with the civilians.

German has been a compulsory part in the school curriculum and adult learning classes have also been formed. German traffic laws have been promulgated. The right hand driving law is enforced. Cars, motorcycles and some bicycles have been confiscated by the forces. Radios also have been taken away, local art treasures have been placed under German protection.

This report is supplementary to the information found in the Nazi's controlled Guernsey Press some of which have reached England. German films and propaganda newsreel are continually shown at local cinemas. People everywhere are requested to bring the correct money owing to shortage of change. Currency is now mainly in German Reichmarks which is valued at just over 2/- (two shillings).'

LIFE ON THE ISLANDS

This is the state of things in Guernsey, as revealed by a special correspondent of the *Lancashire Daily Post*:

The Germans have turned the Island into a gigantic fortress. To this end they have imported millions of tons of cement and completely changed the landscapes familiar to thousands of holiday-makers in pre-war days. Hundreds of houses and greenhouses have been dynamited to make way for the fortifications and given the guns a clear field of fire. In 1941 and 1942 there was an average of 20,000 imported foreign workers engaged on the construction of fortifications, with a German labour corps of 10,000. The foreign workers were French, Belgian, Dutch, Spanish and Russian. Their number is now down to about 7,000 with a labour corps of 3,000.

The garrison troops are estimated at 7,000 against 30,000 in the first two years of occupation. Guns of all calibres up to 16" are mounted on the Island. The firing of the larger guns in practice has brought down hundreds of chimney pots and smashed thousands of panes of glass in the remaining glasshouses. All the quarries are still working at capacity to provide stone for the fortifications.

In Guernsey, as on the mainland, the chief interest is in food, clothing and fuel. Conditions are not much better than in Greece and other parts of Europe. The bread is composed of bran, wood-pulp and a proportion of flour. The ration is 6 lb per week for men labourers and 4½ lb for women workers. The ordinary adult ration is 4 lb with 3 lb for a child. The official meat ration is 4–6 lb a fortnight but usually there is none. For a period of six months, no meat at all was available. A considerable amount of seaweed (carrageen moss) is being eaten.

A Typical Daily Menu:

Breakfast of one slice of bread. Lunch of ¾ lb potatoes and carrots or other vegetables boiled in sea-water because no other salt is available. Tea is 1½ slices of bread with boiled seaweed and milk if any is available.

Tea, coffee etc are virtually non-existent; £8 was paid for ¼ lb packet of tea. There has been some macaroni during the present year. The plight of the Islanders this winter is likely to be bad. The potato crop suffered from the bad summer weather and the fuel position is becoming worse.

The occupying troops have behaved reasonably well and reports suggest that the two commandants who 'ruled' the Island up to mid-summer showed the Islanders consideration. A new commandant who took over a few months ago however, is not so favourably reported upon. What has horrified the Islanders has been the treatment of the foreign slaves. They were landed in a starving condition, their only clothing being cement bags. They were whipped at their work and sometimes dropped dead. The dead were simply thrown into a lorry and tipped over the rubbish dump at the Vale Castle.

The Nazis have made some efforts to 'Germanise' the Islands. Streets have been renamed. High Street is Haugh Strasse, Doyle Road has become Doyle Strasse and so on. German is taught in the schools. Churches and chapels are allowed to function as usual, except that no singing of the National Anthem is permitted. Wireless receivers are banned but a certain amount of news leaks into the Island in spite of the poor communications. Cinemas are still open, showing all German films.

Waiting List for Prison.

Minor offences keep prisons full. Convicted persons remain free until cell available, then get card to come and serve sentence. Extensions granted to farmers at harvest time. Channel Islanders, Huns and alien labourers don't mix. Aliens have hardest life.

In a police court case, one Bert Richings, a shopkeeper, was charged with using electric current during the prohibited hours and heavily fined. Also a woman, Florence Simon, was heavily fined for procuring bread in excess of her ration.

Newspaper reports later did not help with headlines on the mainland: 'Channel Islanders on Starvation Diet and Disease Ridden'. One newspaper, *The Sunday Despatch*, as early as August 1940 published an article written by a man who had escaped from Guernsey claiming all the women were being placed in concentration camps and were already near starvation. What terrible news to read at this time as there was no way one could find out any news of loved ones. The very first service to be severed from the Islands were telephone calls to the mainland.

When paper was available during 1941, a monthly journal for Channel Island refugees in Great Britain was published by the Stockport and District Channel Island Society. Many contributed to it and many showed their yearnings to get back to the Islands.

Our Guernsey anthem I am sure was always song at The Channel Island Society meetings when held – it has always been a song that brings tears to our eyes, especially emotional and at times such as the war years, this song and tune would have a special meaning and was printed in the journal along with the poems:

SARNIA CHERIE

First verse

Sarnia, dear homeland, gem of the sea,
Island of beauty, my heart longs for thee,
Thy voice calls me ever, in waking or sleep,
Till my soul cries in anguish, my eyes ache to weep,
In fancy, I see thee, again as of yore,
Thy verdure clad hills and thy wave beaten shores,
Thy rock sheltered bays, ah, of all thou art blest,
I'm returning to greet thee, dear Island of rest.

Then follows the meaningful words of the chorus which all Guernseymen and women love.

CHORUS

Sarnia Cherie, Gem of the Sea,
Home of my childhood, my heart longs for thee,
Thy voice calls me ever, forget thee I'll never,
Island of Beauty, Sarnia Cherie.

Second Verse

I left thee in anger, I knew not thy worth,
Journey afar, to the ends of the earth,
Was told of far countries, the heav'n of the bold,
Where the soil gave up diamonds, silver and gold,
The sun always shone, and race took no part,
But thy cry always reached me, its pain wretched my heart,
So I'm coming home, thou of all art the best,
Returning to greet thee, dear Island of rest.

Then repeat the Chorus once more, even louder I'm sure and with great gusto!

IN ANOTHER *CHANNEL ISLAND REVIEW*, MR BAGGS, A FORMER
MASTER OF VAUVERT SCHOOL WROTE, ALSO IN 1941:

Golden sands and happy pleasance,
Under broad and sunny skies,
Ever smiling, even offering,
Radiant hints of paradise,
Now though grimly striving, trusting,
Sun shall yet break through the rain,
Evening grey shall turn to morning,
Yester-days will dawn again.

PATIENCE STRONG WROTE THIS POEM PUBLISHED IN THE
DAILY MIRROR ENTITLED 'TO A CHANNEL ISLANDER'.

All these poems must have given many Islanders comfort.

God scattered a handful of gems in the sea,
The Islands where men were once happy and free,
Loyal were the people and fair was the land,
Now in the grip of an enemy hand,
Weep for their sorrows, remember and pray,
For the bright dawn of that glorious day,
When once again there'll be singing and smiles,
And you will return to the Beautiful Isles.

To Exiled Islanders

Christmas 1943
Have Faith! dear heart
Again the bells shall ring
Once more the angels sing
And peace again shall reign

Be Brave! dear heart
However dark the days
How sad may be your ways
The sun shall shine again

Trust yet! dear heart
That all your anxious fear
For those you hold so dear
Shall vanish with the year

Until you greet that day
The dawn of which we pray
We feel for you and say
Be brave, have faith dear heart

Walter J Champion

Our Lifeline

The Red Cross Messages Begin and Letters from Germany

My family all stayed together in Guernsey so we did not have the concern of separation to worry about, although we were all (especially my mother) really frightened to leave the house after the Germans arrived. I have said many times when I give talks, I truly believe the month of June 1940 was one of the most worrying for all Islanders and the most upsetting month of the war because of the evacuation.

Therefore, it was with great relief that the International Red Cross made contact and organised the despatch and delivery of forms with Red Cross messages arriving in the UK from the Islands early in 1941. However, messages could take anything up to four or five months to arrive with no news what ever in between.

I must tell you a little of the International Red Cross. They started its letter scheme in December 1939 when a short family message could be sent to a relative. At first, the scheme operated only from the UK to some European countries. Then, a godsend, the Channel Islands were included in December 1940. Only 10 words per letter were allowed, then 20 which was finally increased to 25 after a time.

Then quite a procedure had to be undertaken. The local Red Cross bureau would send the forms to the Red Cross Headquarters in London. They were then sent to the GPO for censoring before being taken by sea to Portugal. From Lisbon, they went by train or sea, via Marseille to Geneva where they were inspected by the International Red Cross officials and stamped with a cachet before being sent to the German Red Cross in Berlin. Not finishing the journey yet, as from Germany they went to Paris, where there was more censoring before they arrived in the Islands. I have wondered how many miles this would have taken! By the end of 1941, the Germans allowed messages from Islanders to be sent monthly, many taking the opportunity to send. Work (as you can imagine) involved a major task in the Red Cross offices on the mainland and many workers were involved in all these countries.

When a message arrived for a local person, a card from the Controlling Committee would be sent to you (see next page) then you would call to receive the message, you could if you wished answer on the back. Staff at 38 High Street would also type out the messages and at other times, there was an office in Market Street. The same procedure would happen on the mainland.

The Controlling Committee of the 967
States of Guernsey.

61.

————— 17 SEP 1941 —————

A communication for you, has been received through the
International Red Cross, from *Marion. Snvaldsen.*

If you will call at 38, High Street, between 10 a.m. and
12.30 p.m. on any morning, or between 2 p.m. and 4.30 p.m. on any
afternoon (except Thursday), you can see the communication and send
a reply not exceeding 25 words.

Please reply to this notice immediately. Even if you do not wish
to answer the communication, let the Red Cross Department know or
you will delay the return of many messages.

GEO. A. BRADSHAW,
Red Cross Department.

IMPORTANT.—Please bring this Card with you.
CAMP DU ROI PRINTING WORKS

There was a charge of one shilling (or 5p now) to send a message out, but money
was well spent as these precious messages were shown to other Guernsey children
at schools and then read out at the Channel Island Society meetings, which were
held around the country. One can imagine how wonderful it was to hear from loved
ones here, because living on an Island in a small community, many knew each other
and families. Any news was good to hear and likewise when messages arrived in
Guernsey, the word soon got around, especially with the wording of all messages
printed locally in the *Star*, our newspaper. Columns of engagements, weddings,
births, 'thank yous', deaths etc. were frequently published for all to read. Likewise, the
Channel Island monthly reviews produced and sold to evacuees (and those abroad)
with messages regarding Islanders and those living in all areas of the mainland and
beyond. Certainly worth the 4*d.* charged (sent by post 5*d.* and 2/6 subscription for
six months) having 144 pages crammed with news, many were delighted to buy it at
the meetings held frequently. Some articles printed in this book were based on information from reports in *The Times, Daily Telegraph, Daily Mail, News Chronicle,
Observer, Sunday Express* and *News of the World* and also information given to
Channel Island Societies meetings by the Guernseymen who escaped from the island.

Another article from a newspaper –

'In Guernsey, German is taught in all schools. No one is allowed on the White
Rock. The beaches are mined. Fishing is permitted under escort. Those who work
for the Germans have extra pay. The Germans are very thorough and if they say
they will do a thing they will do it!'

How right this correspondent was! As you will see, most Red Cross letters sent
were of a personal and loving nature and with local and family news. Although
heavily censored, some got through and were sent with code messages such as:

'MORRIS LEFT US' = the Germans had taken the family car.

'GERAULD NOW LIVING IN YOUR HOUSE' = Germans had taken over the readers home and Gerauld being 'Jerry' (meaning German).

'OFTEN HEAR FROM JACK WARNER' = listening to the BBC Radio.

'LITTLE PYE DEAD, VERY SAD' = radio confiscated or radio broken.

Many messages mentioned 'MRS HUBBARD' as in Old Mother Hubbard and her empty cupboard. Another 'NO NEWS GEORGE, ELIZABETH', implying Islanders could not listen to the news.

A message from a young man who stayed in the Island sent a message to his parents telling them he hoped to be with 'TOMMY' or 'JACK' soon. As they knew no one of these names, they took it he was hoping to be free soon to join the Forces.

Some 2,000 deportees from the Islands who were in internment camps in Biberach, Laufen and Wurzach (southern Germany) could write a fairly long letter on a special double postcard which could easily be opened and censored before reaching their family and friends in the Islands.

Cards could also be sent from Germany to UK mainland addresses, and visa versa so these in turn would give news of those on the mainland to the Internees and then on to friends and family on the Islands.

Dowding Letters

It must have been a wonderful surprise for Mrs A. M. Romeril, (who evacuated from Guernsey in 1940 to Cardiff) to receive a wedding photograph of her niece and husband who had married in Guernsey. John and Dorothy Dowding married in October 1943 and Norman Grut (from the Gruts shop in Guernsey) was allowed to take an inside (only) photograph of the wedding. The newlyweds were naturally thrilled with being allowed this and dearly wanted their relations on the mainland to see it.

At the time, Mrs Dowding was working at the *Guernsey Press* and with her worked a colleague, Mr T. L. Loftus, who unfortunately, because he was English born, was one of many who were deported to internment camps in Germany. When writing to him in Laufen camp, she enclosed the wedding photo. He then sent it on for his wife and his daughter, Juliet who had evacuated in 1940 and had settled in York. From York, Mrs Loftus posted the photo on to Mrs Dowding's aunt and when replying by the Red Cross message to Dorothy and John, she spoke of 'unbelievable joy' at seeing the wedding family group. That was surely a special photograph to receive at the time.

The following Red Cross letter was sent by Mr John Dowding to his niece Ruth with his reply (both with private meaning messages)

'ALL YOUR TOYS SAFE IN CUPBOARD' = meant home in Well Road, Guernsey intact.

'PILOT GONE BUT HAVE SMALLER DOG' = meant large radio gone but a smaller set in its place.

'IS DADDY WITH SAME FIRM' = meant is Daddy still in RAF?

Young niece 'Angel' replied in own handwriting.

PMC      R.C.B.GUERNSEY.

A   32956

Deutsches Rotes Kreuz
Präsidium / Auslandsdienst
Berlin SW 61, Blücherplatz 2

ANTRAG

an die *Agence Centrale des Prisonniers de Guerre, Genf*
— Internationales Komitee vom Roten Kreuz —
auf Nachrichtenvermittlung

REQUÊTE

*de la Croix-Rouge Allemande, Présidence, Service Étranger
à l'Agence Centrale des Prisonniers de Guerre, Genève
— Comité International de la Croix-Rouge —
concernant la correspondance*

1. Absender   John Dowding. 5 Well Road. GUERNSEY.C.I.
   Expéditeur

bittet, an

prie de bien vouloir faire parvenir à

2. Empfänger   Miss Ruth Dowding. R.C.B. 565. Victoria
   Destinataire   Hall. Rolleston St. Salisbury.WILTS.
   ENGLAND.

folgendes zu übermitteln / *ce qui suit :*

(Höchstzahl 25 Worte!)   PASSED
(*25 mots au plus!*)   P.277

All your toys safe in cupboard. Pilot gone,
but have smaller dog. Is Daddy with same
firm? Are you progressing at school?
Birthday Greetings. Love.

(Datum / *Date*)   1.3.43. 8 AVR. 1943   (Unterschrift / *Signature*)

3. Empfänger antwortet umseitig
   Destinataire répond au verso

003899   -7 JUL 1943

Deutsches Rotes Kreuz
Briefstempel
Beauftragte...

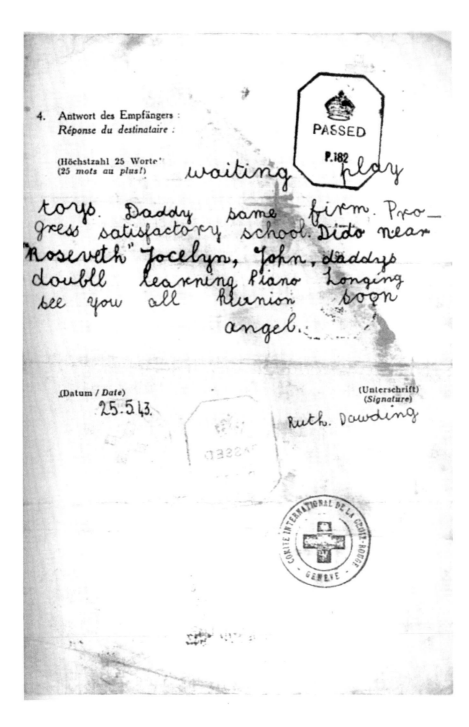

4. Antwort des Empfängers :
   Réponse du destinataire :

(Höchstzahl 25 Worte)
(25 mots au plus!)

PASSED
P.182

waiting play toys. Daddy same firm. Progress satisfactory school. Dido near "Roseveth" Jocelyn, John, daddys double learning Piano Longing see you all reunion soon angel.

(Datum / Date)
25.5.43.

(Unterschrift)
(Signature)

Ruth. Dawding

Those inter news letters helped many with concerns on both sides as there was little one could say in 25 words. Writing letters was also allowed between the Internees in the camps and this surely must have helped having contact with one another. Censorship could be quite severe but other messages were evidently not read at all.

The wedding photograph of Mr and Mrs J. Dowding that travelled to Laufen camp and within the U.K.

THE DAME OF SARK, LETTERS FROM GERMANY

The Dame of Sark, Mrs Sibyl Hathaway, like many others, knew the sadness of seeing her husband, Robert, having to leave Sark in February 1943. The Channel Islanders were again to be punished for a commando raid on Sark and more were to be deported to Germany. Some 63 persons with ages ranging from 8 to 70 would have to go.

Unfortunately, the Dame's husband was among them as he had held a commission and was an officer in the First World War. Included in this number were also women and children, all of whom the Dame must have known, and like in Guernsey when they all left together, there was great worry and concerns at the harbours.

Robert Hathaway, with other men was taken to Laufen and was at the Internment camp for two and a half years. At first, the Hathaways wrote to each other weekly, the Dame receiving news of her friends and family in Robert's letters. She was sending open letters to her husband through the German Feldpost and he would send the camp cards or letters to her with many times in their particular pre-arranged code form, which only the immediate family would be able to understand, such as:

'BUZZ', a one time Seigneurie cat, represented the British and United States Forces.

'LENFRANCIES' or 'FRANKYS', an Italian friend – represented the Italians.

'STEWART', Bob's brother – represented the United States Forces.

'HARRY', Harry Cantan, Amice's army husband – represented the British army.

'RALPH', Ralph Meek an RAF friend from Cologne days or Buster's Firm – represented the Royal Air Force.

'PAT', Pat Horan a British naval officer married to one of Sibyl's friends from Ross-on-Wye days – represented the Royal Navy.

'BELLA' or 'BEAU', Sibyl's French poodles – represented France or French.

'LULU', a German woman friend – represented the Germans.

'MORTIMER' represented electricity or power because they called a favourite old sewing machine 'Mortimer'.

Internierungslager　　　Datum: Aug. 3. 1943.

Post card only this week - Letters from M and J. no news but all well. Writing J. to accept trip to Scotland (clothes fares etc) as present from me. Received blue pyjamas, grape fruit-sticks - butter. Please send large long stem Dunhill pipe (top drawer trunk) old leather cigarette case (basket dressing table). butter good but please substitute with jam and honey - any ammount - have PLENTY of pumps - soap. Send leather golf jacket to re-place worn out tweed coat, then with flannell trousers to come from you, NO more clothes of any kind needed. Letter next week. All my love to you and can never thank you for all you do for me. My love to all as ever. Bless your heart

It was interesting to see Robert Hathaway's requests were mainly for honey, jam and onions but luckily on two occasions, the Dame managed to send small bottles of whisky or brandy which she labelled 'Sleeping Draught' and which the Germans passed through to him!

Letters printed with kind permission of Caroline Bell, the granddaughter of Dame Sibyl and of Barbara Stoney, author of *Sibyl, Dame of Sark*.

Oct. 5. 1943 – Letter only this week. Yours Sept 15 last received and hope you enjoyed Symonds. No more news from Eng since I last wrote to you. Your plum jam is wonderfull, and onions always welcome. Keightley has joined our room, making eight in all. I am glad to have him, as he has been to Canada (etc) and understands my particular brand of U.S.A. humor. Am attending a series of lectures on agriculture given once a week by Wynne - very interesting, and start a series soon by Keightley on heating. All well and very good spirits here. Warn Bennett when phone system repaired Seigneurie MUST be no 1, doctor 2 (etc) important PLEASE. Jehanne sending more shirts, socks (etc) - have everything I need now - lighter and what came in onions MUCH appreciated. No Allright letter. Love to them, Ann

and all others. Am well and the days slip by approaching the party. All my love as always to you and you will never know how happy you have made me with your constant kindness and care. I think of nothing but you and bless you all the time. My constant thoughts are always with you as ever - All my love to you always

RED CROSS MESSAGES

Re-living Guernsey's life-line with the outside world during Guernsey's Occupation, 1940–1945. Messages of few words that meant so much and the wonderful gift of food parcels which arrived by the *Vega* during the last five months, saving many lives.

I have been privileged to read many Red Cross messages between families and friends, and many especially loaned by Mr Neville Robilliard. He went away at the age of two and a half with his mother, Elsie, whilst his father Nicholas, stayed. His father wrote in his diary that they left at 1pm on June 21st 1940. Neville's sister, Lois (who was aged seven and a half at the time), had left at 3am on the same day with other children from Torteval School. She later passed a scholarship to the Intermediate School, then staying at Rochdale with other pupils.

Many messages went back from and to Guernsey, Chester, Rochdale and Lancashire and then Manchester where Neville and his mother stayed, living with a doctor and Mrs Heywood, who Neville tells me, were wonderful to them all. They were indeed very lucky. These messages showed much concern and love for each other and their children and family.

I believe schoolchildren were the very first to be allowed to send a message home to a parent. The teachers probably helped Lois and others too (see Marion Petit's first message later on). The very first message of ten words were sent from Elsie:

'Dear Nic, We are fine, trust you are same.'

Sent November 1940, received in Guernsey March 31st, 1941 nine months after leaving Guernsey to hear any word from Elsie and the children!

Lois wrote:

'Happy, have good clothing, don't worry, mother alright. Love Lois.'

Ten words sent November 11th 1940, received February 21st 1941. Her father received this message on February 21st, being eight months since he waved Lois goodbye.

From :

WAR ORGANISATION OF THE BRITISH RED CROSS
AND ORDER OF ST. JOHN

To :

Comité International
de la Croix Rouge
Genève

Prisoners of War,
Wounded and Missing
Department

ENQUIRER
Fragesteller

Name .... **ROBILLIARD.**

Christian name .... **NEVILLE (MASTER)**
Vorname
Address .... **RED CROSS MESSAGE BUREAU.**

No. **7 5 1,**

GADDUM HOUSE, 16, QUEEN ST.,

MANCHESTER, 2, ENGLAND.

Relationship of Enquirer to Addressee .... **SON**
Wie ist Fragesteller mit Empfänger verwandt?

The Enquirer desires news of the Addressee and asks that the following
message should be transmitted to him.
Der Fragesteller verlangt Auskunft über den Empfänger. Bitte um Weiter-
beförderung dieser Meldung.

DARLING DADDY,   I'M GROWING, NOT SO CHUBBY.

I REMEMBER RAYMOND, MR. CAMP. LOVE TO GRAN

GRANPA.   SEE YOU SOON.

NEVILLE.

PASSED

P.121

Date .... **14th July, 1941**

ADDRESSEE
Empfänger

Name .... **ROBILLIARD.**

Christian name .... **NICHOLAS (MR)**
Vorname
Address .... **LE DOUVRE.**

TORTEVAL.

GUERNSEY.   CHANNEL ISLANDS.

The Addressee's reply to be written overleaf.
Empfänger schreibe Antwort auf Rückseite.

15 SEPT. 1941

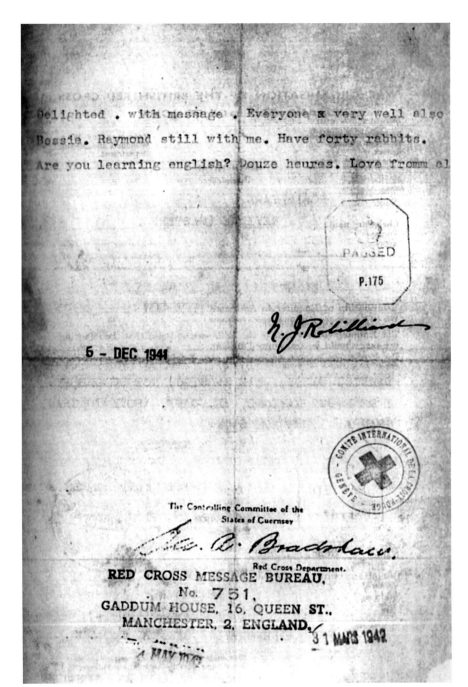

Delighted . with message . Everyone x very well also
Bessie. Raymond still with me. Have forty rabbits.
Are you learning english? Douze heures. Love fromm el

PASSED
P.175

E. J. Robilliard

5 - DEC 1941

The Controlling Committee of the
States of Guernsey

RED CROSS MESSAGE BUREAU,
No. 751,
GADDUM HOUSE, 16, QUEEN ST.,
MANCHESTER, 2, ENGLAND,
Red Cross Department.

31 MARS 1942

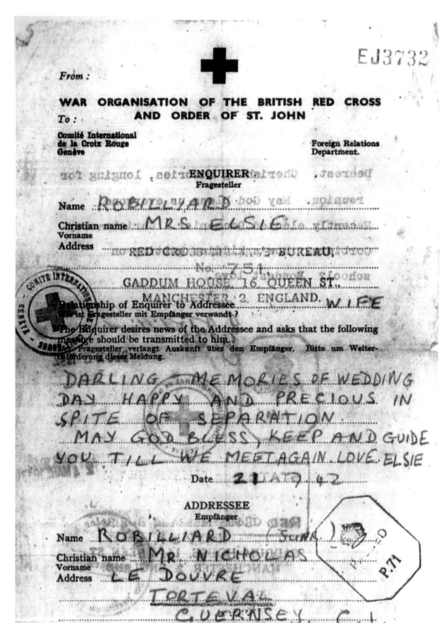

EJ3732

From:

**WAR ORGANISATION OF THE BRITISH RED CROSS
AND ORDER OF ST. JOHN**

To:

Comité International
de la Croix Rouge
Genève

Foreign Relations
Department.

ENQUIRER
Fragesteller

Name ROBILLYARD

Christian name MRS. ELSIE
Vorname

Address RED CROSS BUREAU
No. 751
GADDUM HOUSE 16 QUEEN ST.
MANCHESTER 2. ENGLAND. WIFE

Relationship of Enquirer to Addressee.
Wie ist Fragesteller mit Empfänger verwandt?
The Enquirer desires news of the Addressee and asks that the following
message should be transmitted to him.
Der Fragesteller verlangt Auskunft über den Empfänger. Bitte um Weiter-
beförderung dieser Meldung.

DARLING MEMORIES OF WEDDING
DAY HAPPY AND PRECIOUS IN
SPITE OF SEPARATION
MAY GOD BLESS KEEP AND GUIDE
YOU TILL WE MEET AGAIN LOVE ELSIE

Date 21 MAY 42

ADDRESSEE
Empfänger

Name ROBILLIARD (SINA)
Christian name MR NICHOLAS
Vorname
Address LE DOUVRE
TORTEVAL
GUERNSEY C.I.

The Addressee's reply to be written overleaf. (Not more than 25 words).
Empfänger schreibe Antwort auf Rückseite. (Höchstzahl 25 worte).

AOUT 1942

WAR ORGANISATION OF THE BRITISH RED CROSS
AND ORDER OF ST. JOHN

Dearest. Cherishing memories, longing for
reunion. May God bless us everyone.
Recently elected Douzenier. ChristmasDay
Corbiere. How's kiddies getting on
school? Bondest love.

R. J. Robilliard

DEC 28 1942

STATES OF GUERNSEY

RED CROSS MESSAGE BUREAU
GADDUM HOUSE, 16, QUEEN ST.,
MANCHESTER, 2. ENGLAND

1943 – 'Frank and Joe' were mentioned by Nic. 'Frank Phillips was a news-reader' but for Joe, Neville has no recollection as a friend or family by the returned message, a photograph did get through to 'Nic' and with Sandy mentioned – Sandy Macpherson was regularly on the radio as a well-known organist. You will see that Elsie forwarded the photograph through writing to Rev Foss – then on to Nicholas, which must have been lovely to receive,

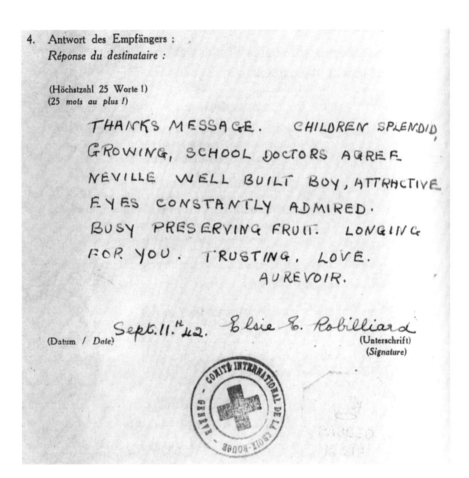

Other messages were of concern for each other and how are the children? Nic was keen for Lois to take music lessons and what is the height of the children, etc etc, always looking forward to the reunion but keeping his chin up.

Again on January 13th 1945:

> 'Elsie Dearest. All very well. New Year as usual, hope wishes be realised. Spending much time with 'Frank and Joe' – good companions. Longing for reunion. Love Nic.'

States Emergency Hospital
Castel , Guernsey .
1·3·9·43

Dear Mr Robilliard .

My father in Germany , has received a letter from your wife enquiring after you and your parents , and enclosing the enclosed photograph .

She also writes — " Tell me we are very well and live in hope for that great day . Can you tell me about my father's last illness ? Was he able to see his grandchild ? How is mother and sister ? Do you know anything of Helene , is she well and what has become of her . Ruth is well , enjoying life , has recently left for an unknown destination ; still nursing "

Father is sorry he has not enough letter forms to be able to write to ~~him~~ you personally , so he asked me to pass the message on to you . If you would like to reply his address is

INTERNIER TEN POST
Rev H. J . Foss .
9986 B 2/20
INTER NIERUNGS LAGER
BIBER ACH /RISS
DEUTSCH LAND.

Kindest regards to you all ,

Yours sincerely

Enid M . Foss .

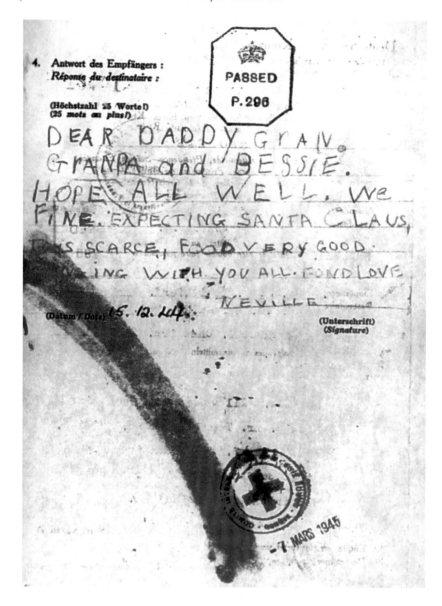

Messages did not always pass the censors as you will see one copied here. The last letter from Neville would have been one of the favourites to dad I'm sure, received in March 1945.

I expect when Neville, Lois and Mum returned, they would have heard how their dad made a crystal set so he could listen to the news every day to Sandy's organ playing like they all used to do and to Frank Phillips.

Apparently, when Nicholas made a crystal set, he managed to have two sets of ear phones. There was a young German who one day asked if he could leave his bicycle in Nicholas's shed as he felt if it was left outside it would get damaged or taken over-night by others. He was allowed to do this, and in time, getting to know him a little, and confident he could be trusted they used to listen to the news together!

He was friendlier than one whom Nicholas saw one day helping himself to carrots from a field nearby. This German had a sack and was happily collecting between the rows until Nicholas gave a shout and told him to 'Clear off and leave the carrots alone'. Well the German did make a dash but the sack had a hole in it and carrots were falling from it along the fields and with that, Nicholas was picking them up and throwing them at the German. But when the German hit the main road, he'd had enough of it and turned around, directing a revolver straight at Nicholas! It was now Nicholas's turn to clear off rather quickly!

- Red Cross Letters -

Marion Petit

Many of the letters I have seen although of a few words, they just express the heartache of separation, especially between parents and children. None more so than of Marion Petit (nee Enevoldson) whom I had the pleasure of meeting recently. She evacuated in 1940 with pupils from St Andrews School after going to the school with her mother three times. Her parents felt, like so many others, that they would follow on later but because their older folk, the grandparents, did not intend to leave, they felt they had best stay for them. Marion, an only child, travelled on the ship *Viking* and a coincidence her husband, Cyril, was also on the same boat but had not known each other at this time. She travelled, with the St Andrews School, by train from Weymouth to Manchester. After a short stay she went to a church at Eccles and finally ended up at the Village Hall at Irby. She felt the kind helpers at the hall weren't quite sure where the children had come from (she thinks France) as they had made a large urn of black coffee for them! You can imagine the offer did not receive much excitement!

Marion was ten and a half years old at this time and because of her age, she was a preferred choice to live with a Mr and Mrs Boumphrey who had a little boy of 18 months, whom Marion got very fond of. She quickly fitted in with this nice family and helped with the little boy, Brian. In 1944, another baby, Ian, was born so Marion was in her element helping out again.

Marion's first letter which was written by a teacher to mum and dad, was in November 1940 when only ten words were allowed and was received in April 1941 with a reply made soon after. In all, Marion has kept all thirty-five loving letters between her and her parents. She left school at fourteen and started work as a pastry cook. On arrival, remarks from other workers told her 'You won't be long working here as the British has landed in France – it's D-Day and the Islands will soon be free of Germans.' Well, it was longer than everyone thought and it was thirteen months before Marion set foot in Guernsey again.

On telling me of the first glance of her mum and dad on arrival, she shed tears remembering how they looked – thin and shabbily dressed, not how she remembered them. They too had forgotten she was five years older and almost sixteen. They thought of her as she had left, a child. Marion had hoped she would come home and have a baby brother or sister to look after, as she really missed her family back at Irby. She was very disappointed.

COMITÉ INTERNATIONAL DE LA CROIX-ROUGE

Palais du Conseil Général

GENÈVE (Suisse)

61

C. M. I. 4855/1.

DEMANDEUR — ANFRAGESTELLER — ENQUIRER

Nom - *Name* *Enevoldsen*

Prénom - *Christian name* - *Vorname* *Miss M².*   654

Rue - *Street* - *Strasse* *B. R. C. and St John War Organisation*
Bureau 201 - St James's Palace

Localité - *Locality* - *Ortschaft* *London*

Département - *County* - *Provinz* .·..

Pays - *Country* - *Land* *England.*

Message à transmettre — Mitteilung — Message

(25 mots au maximum, nouvelles de caractère strictement personnel et familial) —
(*nicht über 25 Worte, nur persönliche Familiennachrichten*) – (*not over 25 words,
family news of strictly personal character*).

Very happy comfortable
thinking of you. Merry
christmas love

Marion

Date - *Datum* *Nov. 40.*

DESTINATAIRE — EMPFÄNGER — ADDRESSEE

Nom - *Name* *Enevoldsen*

Prénom - *Christian name* - *Vorname* *M²*

Rue - *Street* - *Strasse* *Homedale - Vauquiedor -*

Localité - *Locality* - *Ortschaft* *St Andrews*

Province - *County* - *Provinz* *Guernsey.*

Pays - *Country* - *Land*

ANTWORT UMSEITIG	RÉPONSE AU VERSO	REPLY OVERLEAF
Bitte sehr deutlich schreiben	Prière d'écrire très lisiblement	Please write very clearly

RÉPONSE   ANTWORT   REPLY

Message à renvoyer au demandeur — Mitteilung an den Aufragesteller
zurückzusenden — Message to be returned to enquirer

(25 mots au maximum, nouvelles de caractère strictement personnel et familial) —
(nicht über 25 Worte, nur persönliche Familiennachrichten) — *(not over 25 words,
family news of strictly personal character).*

Dear Marion,

November message received, both well.

Always thinking of you. Hope to see

you before long. Keep happy. Love

and kisses.   Mum and Dad.

PASSED P.57

Date:
Datum: APR 3 1941   *C. Envoldson*

The Controlling Committee of
the States of Guernsey.

Geo. A. Bradshaw.

Red Cross Dept.

26 MAI 1941

Bitte sehr deutlich schreiben   Prière d'écrire très lisiblement   Please write very clearly

Deutsches Rotes Kreuz
Präsidium / Auslandsdienst
Berlin SW 61, Blücherplatz 2

R.C.B Guernsey.

3/ 6589

ANTRAG

an die *Agence Centrale des Prisonniers de Guerre, Genf*
— Internationales Komitee vom Roten Kreuz —
auf Nachrichtenvermittlung

REQUÊTE

de la Croix-Rouge Allemande, Présidence, Service Étranger
à l'Agence Centrale des Prisonniers de Guerre, Genève
— Comité International de la Croix-Rouge —
concernant la correspondance

1. Absender Enevoldsen, Homedale, Vauquiedor,
Expéditeur

St. Andrews, Guernsey.

bittet, an
prie de bien vouloir faire parvenir à

2. Empfänger Marion Enevoldson,
Destinataire

c/o St. Andrews Guernsey School,

P.175   Chester.

folgendes zu übermitteln / *ce qui suit* :

(Höchstzahl 25 Worte !)
(*25 mots au plus !*)

Deutsches Rotes Kreuz

Dearest Marion,

Hope well and happy. No message for
a long time. Like to know how you are
getting on at School. Love, Mum, Dad.

Nov. 21st/41.

(Datum / *Date*)

(Unterschrift / *Signature*)

C. Enevoldsen

3. Empfänger antwortet umseitig
Destinataire répond au verso

SHEILA BROWN (NEE REEVE)

To return to the messages, Sheila and her two brothers, left Guernsey with St Martins School, together with their mother who went as a helper. They eventually arrived by train at Stockport. Meanwhile, Roy, the eldest brother, travelled with the Vale School to Scotland and to be all together, was collected and brought back to Stockport. They were indeed fortunate to rent a house owned by the Red Cross.

As you will see by the message, her father stayed on the Island and his message of 'Big Ben' listening to the news managed to get through the censuring.

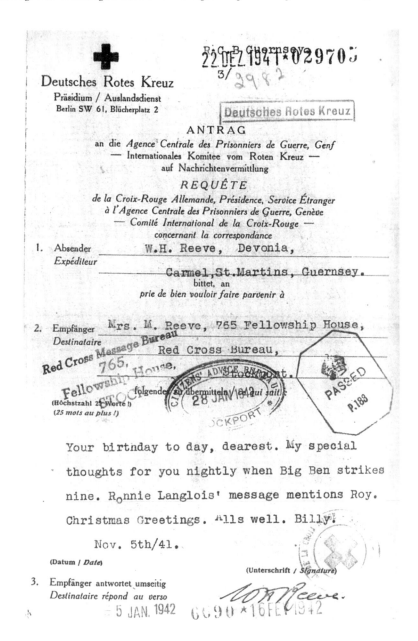

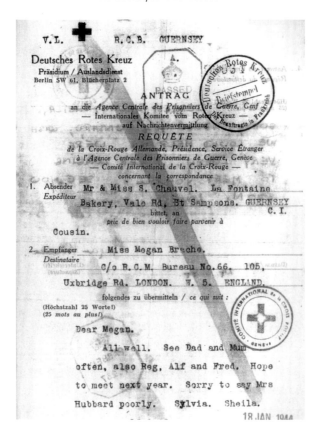

Mr David Pattimore kindly loaned me an envelope which was used apparently over and over again and people who received them were asked to save them and return them to the Bureau. Again, 'Mrs Hubbard' was a popular and well-known lady (although poorly) but Reg, Alf and Fred seemed healthy and got through censoring (R, A and F for the Royal Air Force).

PAT FOREY

Pat Forey from Alderney kindly forwarded me copies and this one printed again mentioned Mrs Hubbard but the answer was censured. I expect she was also poorly, sick or empty, yet again.

My mother, Gladys Finigan, sent this message to my aunt in Manchester in 1942 and back came aunty Kath's letter asking if Ted, Teddy was still with us (Bobby, the younger son evacuated with her). Yes, her husband Ted and son Teddy were living with us as they just could not manage on their own with food shortages etc – hence there were over nine in the family at the time.

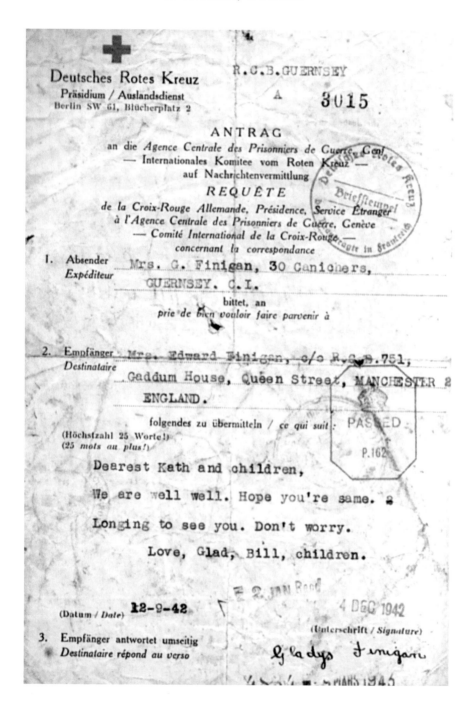

4. Antwort des Empfängers :
   Réponse du destinataire :

(Höchstzahl 25 Worte!)
(*25 mots au plus!*)

DEAR GLADYS
PLEASE TO KNOW THAT ALL
KEEPING well HOPE YOU HAVE
GOT TEd, TEddy STILL wiTH you
BOBBY GETTING quiTE BiG Boy
LOVE KATH

(Datum / *Date*) 20·1·43

(Unterschrift)
(*Signature*)

PASSED

P.172

✚

R 2171

From :

**WAR ORGANISATION OF THE BRITISH RED CROSS
AND ORDER OF ST. JOHN**

552

To :

Comité International
de la Croix Rouge
Genève

Foreign Relations
Department.

ENQUIRER
Frageteller

Name .... LE PREVOST

Christian name .... NELSON H.
Vorname

Address ....

....

....

♔

PASSED

P.182

Relationship of Enquirer to Addressee ....
Wie ist Fragesteller mit Empfänger verwandt ?

The Enquirer desires news of the Addressee and asks that the following
message should be transmitted to him.
Der Fragesteller verlangt Auskunft über den Empfänger. Bitte um Weiter-
beförderung dieser Meldung.

ALL VERY WELL AND HAPPY
SEASON'S GREETINGS. WORKING
TOGETHER. HOW MYRTLE
NELSON.

Date 2·1·11·41

ADDRESSEE
Empfänger

Name .... ROBILLARD

Christian name .... WALTER
Vorname

Address .... SHRUBWOOD
ST. JAQUES.
ST. PETER PORT
GUERNSEY C.I.

The Addressee's reply to be written overleaf. (Not more than 25 words).
Empfänger schreibe Antwort auf Rückseite. (Höchstzahl 25 worte).

30 DEC 1941

Mr N. Le Prevost

Another coded message was sent by Mr N. Le Prevost whose family evacuated. He wanted to know how the family home Myrtle Grove was faring, in St. Jacques. He sent a message to his neighbour and friend and back came the reply – 'Myrtle was engaged' – meaning the Germans had occupied!

On returning in 1945 and really like everyone else wondered what to expect but (like others too) was upset to find their home Myrtle Grove empty of furniture and damaged throughout. All the wooden stair banisters had been ripped out (probably used for firewood) and it was in a sorry state. The authorities had collected what furniture was in houses and stacked in different buildings. With evacuees returning, they were invited to look for their furniture and label what they felt belonged to them but really it was very confusing as Mr Le Prevost found there were many labels on the same items by people claiming they owned the furniture. This decided Mr. Le Prevost and family to return to the mainland and Lloyd (the son) was the only member to return to the Island. He married Enid in Stroud, Gloucestershire in September 1952 and returned to Guernsey soon after.

After recognising Mr. Lloyd Le Prevost through both working at the State's Telephone Department many years ago, it was nice meeting him again and his wife recently when talking of the 'letter' he kindly loaned to me (opposite). Mr Lloyd Le Prevost did mention the state of 'Myrtle Grove' when he and his family came home in 1945, but it wasn't just the condition of the homes found on their return from the mainland that upset families, many returned with mixed feelings and when arriving found other problems to overcome.

The majority were so relieved to be on Guernsey soil again and one can only imagine what it felt like to see and enter the lovely harbour of St Peter Port once more. To arrive early in the morning after such a long time away, would stay in people's minds for always. I am sure there is no other harbour in the world more attractive than ours. One can realise too, how so many evacuees missed the coast and the look and the smell of the sea if they were living inland for five years.

In many cases, in place of this, there was at times unusually cold weather and 'smog' one had to get accustomed to – frightening air raids in the cities and surrounding areas. For children especially, new accents were heard, a dialect which could have sounded like a foreign language to them. Over and above all this, the children that did not attend school with their Guernsey class mates, felt lonely and isolated without their special school friends from home, it was probably a blessing for the Guernsey schools to attend together and to keep together.

I have written about the problems André (my husband) had whilst at school in Wolverhampton and the problems the family had on returning in quite some detail in *Reflections of Guernsey*. Looking for homes and furniture being the main worry. I know that my mother and father helped out one family on returning from the mainland when having nowhere to live. Aunty Edie Masterton and her daughter Betty (now Le Gallez) stayed with us while the rest of their family were living elsewhere, until they managed to get a home together. As a family, they had all evacuated and were all friends before the war began. Many others were forced to share and live in hotels and other places until they had sorted out homes and furniture.

Sadly, there were many children that never really felt close, as they once were, to parents/fathers again, after so long being separated and many did not recognise children/parents, or brothers and sisters the first time they remet. Many like Marion Envoldson's parents could not believe their daughters had grown up and had already started work. We fourteen-year-olds that stayed, were still childish in our outlook, so to speak, but other teenagers had perhaps started working in factories and other work, and grew up very quickly, which made them seem older than their years.

Another friend I have, left at the age of 8 and was fortunate to be living with a very nice family, in a lovely home, with all the luxuries and conveniences, but on returning to her parents, although wanting to see them, she realised home comforts wouldn't be the same as she had been used to. There was no tiled, indoor bathroom and toilet for her now, but an 'earth' toilet was down the garden on their country farm, which she didn't like at all.

Many, after coming home, wandered if they had done the right thing and some returned to their original jobs on the mainland, as apart from the building trade, vinery and greenhouse work, there was little else to choose from.

My dad's sister, Emmie Taylor (I can hardly believe she has recently celebrated her 98th birthday) was evacuated with her three young children, Gene, Lorna and Keith, eventually settled and lived with a very nice family. With both families having children, although crowded, they worked at living together well and were happy. When returning late summer time in 1945, on seeing her husband 'Uncle Alby', she felt as if she was returning from a holiday, but very pleased and relieved to be back with him. Later, they had another son Michael. There were many reasons and many families, when reunited, just could not get on together after such a long separation and many went their separate ways.

Most country children who spoke the Guernsey Patois before they left, naturally lost it after 5 years of not speaking it. That is the reason why so little is heard in the country parishes now. Another Guernsey tradition mostly lost, but now fortunately making a come back and being taught again.

The evacuation and occupation of 1940–1945 surely changed many lives.

Saved by the *Vega*

D-DAY 1944 – WHEN IS THE 'BOAT' COMING?

By August 1944, the Channel Islands were cut off from any foodstuffs or commodities originating from France. In November 1944 due to the seriousness of the situation following the landings of the allied forces, on June 6th on France – the Bailiff was at long last given permission for a message to be sent using the German radio transmitter to the Secretary General of the International Red Cross. Earlier the Bailiff of Guernsey and Mr Victor Carey had asked but had been refused permission to send to the Red Cross for help during 1944. He mentioned the difficulties and shortages and that urgent supplies of essentials was needed urgently. The food and essentials had been in very short supply for quite a while and by November the authorities could see that bread would finish by December 15th, sugar would finish by 6th January, fat reserves by end of January 1945 and milk reduced to 1/3rd pint per head of the population by the end of the year.

Soap and cleansers – completely exhausted. Germans (were hungry too!) were taking the bulk of the vegetables leaving very little available for Islanders, salt stocks finished. Clothing and footwear almost exhausted.

Fuel – gas and electricity – finished by the end of the year and coal stocks exhausted, very little wood available, many medical supplies finished.

Although the Normandy landings seemed successful and news was encouraging, the people of Guernsey were in a desperate state. More so the elderly perhaps living on their own who could not get out to queue and walk looking for food. There were indeed many near to starving, so one can understand spirits were lifted when in late November, it was announced by the German authorities that with talks, a supply of food, soap and medical supplies would be forthcoming. The *Star* announced the great news – such excitement now with the thoughts of relief, but there was another long wait until the Bailiff announced that the ship was due to sail from Portugal on December 7th.

I am sure my mother and father, like thousands of others, were getting really impatient. Every day must have felt like weeks but then, at long last on December 20th an announcement was made saying the ship called *Vega* should be due to arrive on Christmas Day with tons of food! Another wait and we children were so disappointed as no boat arrived on Christmas Day. Everyone had been asking for weeks 'When is the boat coming?' and yet another Christmas passed with little to eat. I can well remember we kept looking out to sea for days on end, our house looked out onto the harbour. She was delayed because they had met stormy seas in the Bay of Biscay and it had been a very rough journey.

The *Vega* *leaving Guernsey waters after unloading her precious cargo* *(Priaulx Library)*

At Long Last

The S.S. *Vega* finally came in on December 27th. I am sure no other ship looked so wonderful and hundreds of people lined the Esplanade to welcome the Red Cross ship with her cargo.

Although our Liberation was an unforgettable day, I have heard it said that the day when the Vega came in was better than being liberated! I can understand this being said as so many people were desperate for food and very cold with no heating. Being a very cold winter, the elderly were in a desperate state. Many more would have died if the boat hadn't come in when it did – she literally just came in time.

Arriving at 5.30pm, it was as the 'boat' we had been waiting for, for so long came into the harbour that everyone gave way to their wrought-up feelings and cheer after cheer went up – the town suddenly came alive and the cheers could be heard all over: '*Vega, Vega!*'

The late Bill Green, a greatly loved and respected Guernsey character and a great friend of ours, recalls the evening when the boat came in and had written:

'As the *Vega* slowly entered the harbour on that moonlit winters evening, all eyes were strained to catch a glimpse of the boat that was going to save the Island from starvation. The *Vega* turned towards the London berth, where she tied up. Suddenly, cheering broke out from the thousands of joyful Islanders who wanted to witness and be part of that historic moment. Ask any Guernsey man, who was in the Island during the occupation, where they were when the *Vega* arrived with its precious cargo of Red Cross parcels and they will tell you precisely. It was one of those moments in our lives that we shall never forget, not even the slightest detail!

While the *Vega* was being unloaded, virtually every Islander went down to the Esplanade to stand and admire and, indeed, pay homage to the ship that had brought us out next meal and our next and our next... the ship that brought us hope, the ship that brought us life.

I stood on the Esplanade and admired the ship, with its Swedish flag proudly flying from its stern and proposed a silent toast; "The *Vega*, God Bless her."'

The parcels were taken from the ship on to the German railway from the White Rock to St. Georges Hall. On New Years Eve, 31st December the long awaited parcels were delivered to the grocers and shortly after we collected one parcel each – some Canadian and some from New Zealand.

I know it was the chocolate that probably we children took delight in but Kaye Le Cheminant has reminded me the New Zealand chocolate had a lovely taste and much preferred to the Canadian. All of the tinned food in the parcels was enjoyed, but many of us had forgotten the taste and perhaps, we had never even had such luxuries before!

There were six visits of the *Vega* and each time she was warmly welcomed by crowds of Islanders. The second visit was on February 7th – she brought parcels for us again which had been eagerly awaited – our food ration for the week 26th February was almost nothing. It was:

> Salt – nil
> Sugar – nil
> Butter and cooking fat – nil
> Meat – nil
> Breakfast foods (oats) – 1½ oz
> Macaroni – 1½ oz
> Potatoes – 5lb
> Milk – 1/3 pint per day.
> Bread – nil

Crates stacked on the quay in Guernsey

Before the food could be unloaded in Jersey a meeting had to be held with:
Left to right: *Baron Von Aufsess; Colonel Iselin of the Swiss army and president of the Red Cross in Lisbon; Attorney General Duret Aubin; Bailiff Coutanche and Colonel Heine*

White Rock, St Peter Port harbour, Red Cross parcels being loaded on the railway to be transported to St George's Hall (Priaulx Library)

(This must have been the week I well remember my mother saying the rations were 2 ½d). One person apparently had her ration of groceries delivered through the letterbox! I have seen the diary kept by Neville Robilliard's father Nicholas Robilliard who lived on his own – every Red Cross message sent and received by him was written down and with each parcel meaning such a lot to him he kept dates, goods, prices of each item and the factory make on the labels. He received a Canadian parcel on Feb 15th and in it was:

5 oz Neilson's chocolate	16 oz Zest Apple and Plum jam
3 ½ ozs Brunswick Sardines	16 oz powdered milk, (KLIM)
7 ½oz Paramount Salmon	4 oz L. H Easterbrooks Tea
4 oz Mapleleaf Cheese	8 oz Sugar
12 oz El Rancho Corned Beef	16 oz McCormick Biscuits
16 oz Mapleleaf Butter	1 oz pepper and salt
7 oz Atlas Raisins	1 tablet Crest soap
6 oz Atlas Prunes	

Total cost 13/9 (approximately 68p!) including packaging.

At other times the diary read 'prisoner's parcel' received on March 3rd 1945 from New Zealand the parcel contained:

8 oz Chocolate
6 oz Tea
14 oz Jam (apple jelly) 'Kirkpatrick's'
10 oz Brown Sugar
14 oz 'Highlander' Condensed milk
13½ oz 'Nestles' coffee and milk
6 oz Sultanas
16 oz New Zealand Dairy Butter
16 oz 'Kai-iwi' cheese
16 oz Corned mutton 'Swifts'
12 oz Lamb and Green Peas 'Swifts'

Total cost 13/6 (approximately 67p!) for everything in parcel and packaging.

It was on this third visit that the *Vega* brought 500 tons flour and no one shall ever forget the first look and taste of this beautiful white bread. We had been without any bread for three weeks and before then the bread really tasted awful – the one given was large round, crispy and they were really delicious! and tasted just like cake. Bakers worked through the night and distribution was made quickly. One doesn't realise the importance of bread until there is none in the shops. It was just an awful time for families and everyone alike.

Mr Irwin Sims (a printer for the *Star* newspaper) also kept a diary of the *Vega*'s arrival dates and for Feb 23rd mentions medical supplies. March 6th mentions NO BREAD. March 7th flour and parcels still being unloaded, we saw the first white loaves for over 4 years! What a sight for people looking in the Fountain Street shops.

24th March – GOOD FRIDAY – lovely hot cross buns made with Red Cross flour at bakehouse (near Grow Ltd). April 5th – *Vega* arrives with flour, sugar, parcels etc. April 15th – We had steamed pudding done to perfection in a 'KLIM' tin!

It seems that the boys from the Castel School found a new pass-time with labels from the parcels, John Trubuil tells me that they had great fun in a collection game called 'Salmon swap' using the different coloured labels they were collecting in the hundreds from the tins! The KLIM tin gave the boys other games. There was 'kick the tin' and turning the two tins upside down , making two holes in each and threading long lengths of string through the holes, they held string then walked on the tins – with practise they even had races! Most of the chocolate came in a tin, which John says was then used for their fags! (The *Vega* brought some cigarettes on later trips, though a gift for the gentlemen!) Mr Robilliard mentions an issue on January 22nd, 10 De Reskes cigarettes and on February 23rd, 40 cigarettes (again in his diary).

It seems the parcels and contents came in for more than one use, but you can see every one was excited each time and looked forward to seeing their special boat arrive.

Collecting parcels in the High Street

S.S. VEGA BROUGHT LETTERS

It was not only food the *Vega* carried. Letters from internment camps in Germany had formerly been carried by the German feldpost but this had ceased from August '44.

On the *Vega*'s last three or four visits she carried Red Cross letters that had accumulated following the allied landings in Normandy, many letters and cards had been held up. These were written by the 2000 internees at Biberach, Laufen and Wurzach to family and friends left in the Islands and were gratefully received after a long wait. Those internees who had a very unhappy and uncomfortable time in the camps were also grateful for the gift of Red Cross food parcels and all the help they had received whilst in Germany and Bavaria. We all had so much to be grateful for during this time.

On the mainland too some families were lucky to have houses to rent from the Red Cross. I have spoken recently to evacuees who, on arriving on the mainland, were eventually housed by the Red Cross. What a blessing that must have been – a roof over their heads!

Within a few hours of the S.S. *Vega* arriving in Guernsey, a Red Cross fund was opened and by October 1945 the total of £40,000 was collected and had been sent to the Duke of Gloucester's Red Cross and St John fund. Quite a large amount at the time, money is still needed for the good work they continue to do all over the world and funds will always be needed

Because of my requests for any interesting Red Cross 'letters', I was pleased and interested to know of one little Guernsey girl who had also raised money for the charity. Rhona Dunn (now Moriarty) was aged four in 1940 when she evacuated with her young brother, Len, and their mother. They settled in Glasgow for the five years and whilst there, young Rhona made little gollies with wool on a backing of cardboard. She was six and a half/seven-years-old at the time and sold these colourful gollies to friends and from knocking on doors selling them for, she thinks 3*d* or 4*d* each! (just less than 1p).

The model of the Vega *made and built by the late Mr Robert Brown*

What an achievement by a little girl! She collected sums of 15/- (75p) in April 1943, £1/16/6 (£1.82) in June 1943 and £1/4/2 (£1.21) in February 1944. Quite a sum in those days and I am sure her father would have been a very proud dad knowing this when the family returned in 1945. He too knew what The Red Cross meant to us all, as he was in the St John Ambulance during the Occupation and was on duty at St George's Hall when the flour arrived on the *Vega*.

After her last visit – the sixth and final on 8th June – on leaving Jersey, the SS *Vega* sailed to London, where she had her Red Cross markings painted out. With fond and grateful remembrance, we shall always remember her. You can see a model of the boat, built by the late Mr Robert (Bob) Brown – a well known Guernseyman, at the German Occupation Museum in the forest. This is well worth a visit.

CITY OF GLASGOW BRANCH, SCOTTISH BRANCH BRITISH RED CROSS SOCIETY.

15 Lynodoch Street, C.3.
1st April, 1943.

This is to certify that permission has been granted to

Name,   Miss Rhona Dunn, (Aged 6),
                    per Mrs. Dunn, (Mother),
Address,   51, Muirhill Avenue, Muirend, Glasgow,

             Make & Sell
To hold,   Golliwogs, etc.,   On   ---------------

on behalf of the Funds of the Glasgow Branch of the Red Cross, registered under the War Charities Act, 1940.

COUNTY DIRECTOR.

Miss C. M. WARREN,
M.B.E.
56 Cleveden Drive, W.2.
(Telephone—Western 283).
County Director.

COUNTY OF THE CITY OF GLASGOW BRANCH
(SCOTTISH BRANCH BRITISH RED CROSS SOCIETY)
TELEPHONE—DOUGLAS 0672
0673

15 LYNEDOCH STREET.

Glasgow, ...17th..June............19 43
C.3.

Miss Rhona Dunn
51 Muirhall Avenue
Muirend
Glasgow.

Dear Rhona,

      Thank you so much for the Red
Cross Box which you brought in on 15th inst.
with money which you have collected from the
sale of Golliwogs which you have made. We
are very grateful indeed for this help which
you have given us for some time now and which
you are carrying on. The Box you brought
in to us on Tuesday contained the splendid
sum of One Pound, Sixteen Shillings and Six
Pence (£1:16:6) and we have sent the money
to our Honorary Treasurer, who will send you
an official receipt.
      We are very sorry that we will
not be able to write you letters of thanks
for the Boxes which you will bring in after
this, because paper is very scarce owing to
the war conditions and we are only writing
to thank people when they send in their first
Box. You will, however, always get an official receipt from our Honorary Treasurer.
      Again thanking you for all you
are doing to help the Sick and Wounded Sailors,
Soldiers and Airmen.

      Yours faithfully,

N. M. Schule

OFFICER IN CHARGE, COLLECTING BOX DEPT.

Miss C. M. WARREN,
M.B.E.
56 Cleveden Drive, W.2.
(Telephone—Western 283)
County Director.

COUNTY OF THE CITY OF GLASGOW BRANCH
(SCOTTISH BRANCH BRITISH RED CROSS SOCIETY)
TELEPHONE—DOUGLAS 0672
                                   0673

15 LYNEDOCH STREET,

Glasgow,............24th February 1944
                  C.3.

Miss Rhona Dunn
35 Largie Road
Glasgow, S.3.

Dear Rhona,

        It was very good of you to make
a collection in aid of the Red Cross and
I am very pleased to be able to tell you
that the Collecting Box which you handed
in on 23rd inst. contained the sum of One
Pound, Four Shillings and Two Pence (£1:4:2).
This money will go to help the sick and
wounded Sailors, Soldiers and Airmen and
we would like to send you our very best
thanks for what you have done for the Red
Cross.
        I have sent the money to our
Honorary Treasurer, who will send you an
official receipt.
        Again with very many thanks.

                Yours faithfully,

                A. M. Shule

                OFFICER IN CHARGE,
        COLLECTING BOX DEPARTMENT.

Mrs Alan Jory at her home in Candie, 9 May 1945

Channel Island Monthly Review, July to December 1943

Three years is such a long, long time;
To leave the ones we loved behind,
We pray, we hope they understand
How we all fare in this strange land.
There isn't much that we can say,
Although we would all gladly pay
The price, no matter what it cost
But courage Sarnians, wear that smile,
We've roughed the worst, it's been worth while,
We've turned the tide, it won't be long,
Our spirits right, our hearts still strong,
Remember – as the boat makes fast –
It's home, our home, we're there at last.

Doris Le Parmentier

Royal Message Sent to Guernsey

Their Majesties, the King and Queen, have sent, through the British Red Cross Society, a congratulatory message to Mr and Mrs J. Wiscombe, of Colyton House, Vale, Guernsey on the occasion of their Diamond Wedding. They were married on October 11th 1883 at the Vale Church.

Every effort was made for the royal message to arrive on or close to the day. What a wonderful message to receive – they must have been delighted, especially under the circumstances.

We children, too were delighted as apparently, after Liberation, the then Princess Elizabeth (now our Queen) sent a gift of honey to every child. It must have been wonderful to spread on our new lovely tasting bread!

Liberation
and Special Poignant Letters from 8–9 May 1945

You will remember in Bill Gillingham's memories, he spoke at the beginning of his dog, Rover, who was put to sleep – hence the message shown here to Bill (1942) and the reply to his sister, brother-in-law and young nephew, Kenny (too faint for publication I am afraid):

'Dearest three. Glad of news. All families here well. Tell Kenny to look after Cobo (their dog). Hoping to see you all soon. Love Mum, Dad, Bill.'

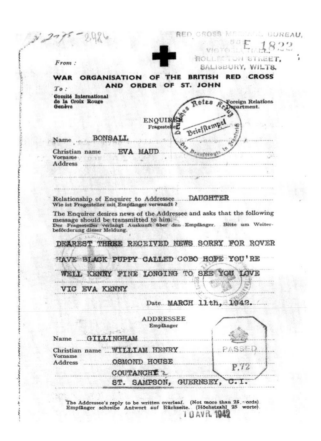

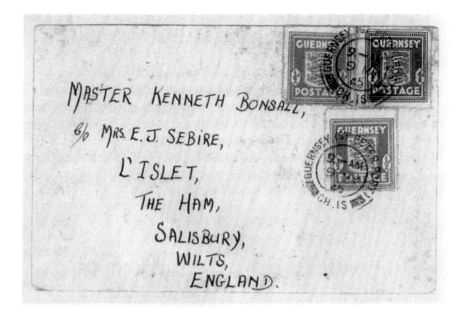

Souvenir of Liberation and Re=Union,
Guernsey, C.I.

MAY 8TH   Correspondence to be Written here.   1945.

Dear Kenny,

I suppose you are a big boy now, although we can only think of you as a baby of 19 months old when you left us, but we hope to see you all very soon. We were all very sorry to see you leave us, but since we have not regretted it but only wished we had all come with you. Anyway that nightmare is over now thank God! We have celebrated V.E. Day in Guernsey to-day, although there are no Allied forces here yet, but we are expecting them tomorrow. Flags are flying everywhere, and every-one is going mad. Will write more tomorrow. It is nearly midnight so I wish you good night. KEEP THIS CARD. BEST WISHES, LOVE, Uncle Bill.

Liberation letter written by 'Uncle Bill Gillingham', May 8th

May. 9. 1945 LAUFEN

Darling girl.
This letter is being delivered by the kindness of the United States army, who came here a couple of days ago an. freed us from the bloody Hun — what a sight to see them speeding down the road toward us — through the front gate and know we were free — and what equipment everything the best and a fine bunch. I am fine, but we do not know how, when, or by what means we are to get home. Tuniston told us yesterday you had been freed, thank heaven for that. Please try and get me back soon by telling Uncle Mark I must return — I think he can have it done by air if you make it strong enough. Also please get one hundred pounds worth of champagne, whiskey, gin, cigarettes and a pound of Dunhill Harmony in case I come direct from here. I go out of the camp now — first time since I got here. food as usual with plenty of Red Cross — we are all well — and such a sight to see our masters under lock and key — the Americans have no nonsense out of them, and God help any S.S. they come across. Well at last the war is over and it took exactly the time you said it would. Do not know when I will write again or whether it is any use for you to write to me — things happen so quickly from day to day. Have heard nothing from Eng for months, but am allowed one other letter beside this one so will drop Mona a line to let the family know all is well. To tell you I am crazy to see you again is useless — have thought of nothing else since I left, and have loved you every minute. My love to the Bishops — Ann. albrights and all — cannot wait to see you all again, but will let you know where I am when I get there. all the love in the world to you and do love everything that you want — keep well and know I think of nothing but you all the time. ... want to see you. Yours always

Bob Hathaway's letter to Sybil from Laufen camp, May 9th

My Aunt's Feelings
sent 8th May 1945

I have written previously in *Reflections of Guernsey* of my Aunt, Mrs Winnie Salmon, who had German soldiers billeted with her throughout the Occupation. Also when we as a family would have to move out the house (an order!) we would always walk up to aunty Win at Shaftsbury House, Havilland Street, St Peter Port. My gran also lived with her and there was an amusing tale about her also in the book.

Aunty Win was my dad's sister and was well loved by the family and I was always pleased to visit her. With regard to her life back in 1934, it was rather tragic even though she had given birth to healthy twins, a boy and a girl. Her husband Bert Salmon, ran a very successful bicycle shop in the town church square where Soundtrack and Joseph's (Hair Salon) shops are now. The basement was then a garage and workshop and on the first floor, he kept accessories and bicycles etc. This was quite a large floor area and he was kept very busy. He was a very well known man in Guernsey and involved with many interests on the Island. Uncle Bert and aunty Win lived in a flat above the shop and had a twin boy and girl, John and Joan aged ten years. It must have been a terribly sad time in 1934 because uncle Bert Salmon (whom I never knew) died the day before aunty Winnie's second twins, Rosemary and Raymond were born.

My dad's other sister, Emmie Taylor (another lovely lady I am very fond of and who also had to cope on the mainland for five years without her husband, bringing up a young family) remembers this very sad time very well and how her sister had to try and cope. She remembers the queues and crowds of people waiting to enter the town church for the service. It was very well attended because he and aunty Winnie were so well known and liked by all. Because aunty Winnie was with the babies in the building opposite the church, no bells rang out at the time.

In 1940, the time of the evacuation, Rosemary and Raymond, now six years old and Joan now 16, left by boat together, John was already on the mainland at a boarding school. John eventually joined the Royal Marines and then trained for the Commandos.

One can imagine how much aunty Winnie missed her children, especially having Germans around her most of the time. Printed here are letters that were sent between them. and from our gran to John. He mentioned this letter his mother had written on May 8th 1945 and it really sums up the whole feeling of being occupied and the heartache of separation. I just had to print it!

My Dearest Children one & all,

How to express my feelings at the present moment I know not. Oh can it be true, an hour ago, the Dear Home of Sarnia was announced free. It is just 4 p.m. the paper has arrived stating we could write at once to our loved ones. Gran & I have immediately (filled with emotion) sat down to do so. Can it be really true, or is it a dream; at last we are out of our Penal Servitude five long weary years under that terrible Nazis Regime & now Freedom, under our Union Jack once again. After the speech this afternoon, out went the flags of Old England in all the neighbouring windows, Uncle Alby & Jack are now busy fixing up one for Shaftsbury. Before I write any further dear, let me inform you all families here are well, that is the news I am longing to receive from you. I cannot write you individually as your address Joan is the one and only I possess. The different feeling I have in my heart already, seems as though you are near me to be able to write these few lines. Will we ever be able to realise it? What we are patiently waiting for now, is to see the arrival of our Glamour boys, which will be after midnight tonight. How we have lived and longed for this great day, only ourselves & the one above knows. It is only hope & faith that has kept us going for this present day, the day of reunion with our loved ones who never (one moment of the day) for five long years has been out of my thoughts & prayers. God has answered my prayers, spared me to see you all again. We speak of and have used the word Freedom in an ordinary, casual way; but never have I realised the meaning & its fullest extent as I have since this German Occupation. When you look through the window and see the different smile on people's faces since 3 p.m. this afternoon, it seems incredible. The huns are still parading the streets, (green flies as we call them) but I expect tomorrow our boys will accompany them. It seems such a coincidence, Our good ship the *Vega* Red Cross arrived in harbour yesterday. We all call her our Saviour, came to us just in the nick of time, but unfortunately too late for many in this Island. Those of us who has survived must thank God. We are all like a lot of school children when we hear at the beginning of the month *Vega* has arrived, but today with this cloud burst, everyone seems to have forgotten their hunger, all so thrilled & keyed up to think we are out of our Concentration Camp. What Gran & I are going to have in a few moments is a cup of real tea, oh how we appreciate a good cup of tea after five years without. When we get our monthly parcel we use our ¼lb. tea very carefully, we stew & stew it over and over again to make it last out. Now darling write me a long letter, & put all the photos possible in same & send on all addresses please. Kiss Ray, John, Rosemary and tell them I am dying for a letter from them all. Also Uncle Ben and Aunty Alice, convey my love to all.

Ever your loving Mum

The Salmon family, late 1940s

Deutsches Rotes Kreuz
Präsidium / Auslandsdienst
Berlin SW 61, Blücherplatz 2

R.C.B.Guernsey.

5/1659

ANTRAG

an die *Agence Centrale des Prisonniers de Guerre*, *Genf*
— Internationales Komitee vom Roten Kreuz —
auf Nachrichtenvermittlung

REQUÊTE

*de la Croix-Rouge Allemande, Présidence, Service Étranger
à l'Agence Centrale des Prisonniers de Guerre, Genève
— Comité International de la Croix-Rouge —
concernant la correspondance*

1. Absender   Mrs. Salmon,

   Expéditeur   Shaftsbury House, Union Str. GUERNSEY.C.I.

   bittet, an
   prie de bien vouloir faire parvenir à

PASSED

2. Empfänger   A.J.B.Salmon,

   Destinataire C/o Gordon. 47. South View Rd.   P.181

             Toughton. ESSEX. ENGLAND.

   folgendes zu übermitteln / *ce qui suit :*

(Höchstzahl 25 Worte !)
(25 *mots au plus !*)

Briefstempel

Darling Boy,
              Hope you're progressing
with Draughtsmanship and keeping well
Family here well. Longing to be with
you all. Fondest love to all family.
              Mother.

(Datum / *Date*)   5th Feb 1942.   W. M. Salmon.
                                    Unterschrift / *Signature*)

3. Empfänger antwortet umseitig
   Destinataire répond au verso

                                    14 AVR. 1942

WATFORD CITIZENS ADVICE BUREAU,
14, HIGH STREET, WATFORD.

From :

WAR ORGANISATION OF THE BRITISH RED CROSS AND ORDER OF ST. JOHN

To :

Comité International
de la Croix Rouge   12/
Genève

I 251

Foreign Relations
Department.

ENQUIRER
Fragesteller

Name .... Salmon.

Christian name .... A.J.B. .
Vorname

Address ....

....

....

Relationship of Enquirer to Addressee .... Son
Wie ist Fragesteller mit Empfänger verwandt ?

The Enquirer desires news of the Addressee and asks that the following message should be transmitted to him.
Der Fragesteller verlangt Auskunft über den Empfänger.   Bitte um Weiter-beförderung dieser Meldung.

    Dearest Mother,

            Received message. Glad you

    are well - Still at School - All family

    well. Aunt Alice sends love - Saw her April

    Keep Smiling Love   *aBSalmon*

            Date.......... 8th May 1942

ADDRESSEE
Empfänger

Name .... Salmon

Christian name .... Mrs.W.M.
Vorname

Address .... Shaftesbury House,
            Union Street,
            Guernsey, C.I.

PASSED
P.191

The Addressee's reply to be written overleaf.   (Not more than 25 words).
Empfänger schreibe Antwort auf Rückseite.   (Höchstzahl 25 worte).

29 MAI 1942

R.C.B. GUERNSEY

Deutsches Rotes Kreuz
Präsidium / Auslandsdienst
Berlin SW 61, Blücherplatz 2

93961

ANTRAG

an die *Agence Centrale des Prisonniers de Guerre, Genf*
— Internationales Komitee vom Roten Kreuz —
auf Nachrichtenvermittlung

REQUÊTE

*de la Croix-Rouge Allemande, Présidence, Service Étranger
à l'Agence Centrale des Prisonniers de Guerre, Genève
— Comité International de la Croix-Rouge —
concernant la correspondance*

1. Absender   Mrs. Brassell,
  Expéditeur
     Shaftsbury House, Union St., GUERNSEY.
          bittet, an   C.I.
    prie de bien vouloir faire parvenir à

2. Empfänger A. J. B. Salmon,
  Destinataire
     R.C.M.B. No 467, Senior School,
     The Avenue, Bushey, WATFORD, HERTS.
                  ENGLAND.

       folgendes zu übermitteln / *ce qui suit :*

(Höchstzahl 25 Worte !)
(*25 mots au plus !*)

Dear John,

    Uncle Jack, I still with Mum.

All well here. Is Uncle Mick writing

you? Longing to see you all. Birthday

Greetings.

           Love - Gran.

(Datum / *Date*)4-8-42.

         (Unterschrift / *Signature*)

3. Empfänger antwortet umseitig
  Destinataire répond au verso

La prumiere ponn'raie a'tamates qui sr'a enviaie souvente la liberation pour Winston Churchill

Martha Martel (nee Hubert)

A chance conversation with Martha (who also stayed with her family) told me of the gift of tomatoes that were sent to Winston Churchill after Liberation. She remembers that her father, a grower, all through the Occupation, would say in Guernsey French 'Winston Churchill will have the very first pickings when we again send tomatoes' and he did of course and back came the reply by telegram (not seen as telegrams today).

Martha also loaned me a red cross letter which was sent to her father from a friend.

44.

```
                                        2nd May,    1946.


The Rt. Hon. Winston L.S. Churchill P.C.  M.P.
Chartwell,
Westerham,
KENT.


Sir,

                It is my great privilege to send you at the
special request of Mr.N.J.Hubert, of Grande Rue, Vale,Guernsey,
who is the grower of the first basket of tomatoes to be produced
this season, the forerunner of the first full season's crop of
tomatoes to be produced since the Occupation of the Island by
the German Forces in 1940.

              .  The Island people will ever remember the occasion
which marked the end of hostilities in Europe, and your speech in
which you mentioned the Liberation of the Islands in such unforgettable
words.

                We hope you will accept this gift as a very small
token of appreciation for all you have done for us.


                        Yours very sincerely,
```

From :

WAR ORGANISATION OF THE BRITISH RED CROSS AND ORDER OF ST. JOHN.

To :

Comité International
de la Croix Rouge
Genève

CROSS MESSAGE BUREAU

No 651

SHORTGWN HALL, BIRMINGHAM.

Foreign Relations
Department.

Expéditeur   SENDER   Absender

Name ...MASON...
Nom
Christian name MR G. B.
Vorname Prènom
Address ....
Adresse
....

PASSED

P.244

MESSAGE   Mitteilung

(Not more than 25 words)   (25 mots au maximum)   (Nicht über 25 Worte)

HAVE SHOWN GUERNSEY PICTURES TO
LARGE CHANNEL ISLANDS SOCIETY
AUDIENCE. ALWAYS IN OUR THOUGHTS
KEEP CHEERFUL   LEAVE A FISH
FOR ETHEL TO CATCH.

G. Bernard

Date Datum... 15. 12. 42.

Destinataire   ADDRESSEE   Empfänger

Name HUBERT,
Nom
Christian name N. J.
Vorname Prènom
Address GRANDE RUE
Adresse
.... VALE
.... GUERNSEY. C.I.

Reply overleaf (not more than 25 words)
Réponse au verso (25 mots au maximum)
Antwort umseitig (nicht über 25 Worte)

Dear Friends,

Hope well. Same at present. Always thinking of old times. Nick fishing summer. Winter greenhouse work. Children keeping cheerful. Longing to meet.

A Hubert

PASS
P.183

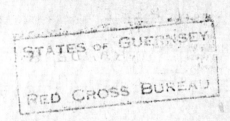

STATES OF GUERNSEY

RED CROSS BUREAU

JUIN 1943

POST OFFICE

TELEGRAM

Charges to pay

s. d.

RECEIVED

From

5 [4p]

m

18

Prefix. Time handed in. Office of Origin and Service Instructions. Words.

To.

118 4.26 LONDON T 30

GUERNSEY TOMATO SHIPPING BOARD PROSPECT HOUSE

LES-BANQUES GUERNSEY =

THANK YOU AND MR HUBERT SO MUCH FOR YOUR VERY KIND

GIFT AND THOUGHT OF ME WHICH I GREATLY VALUE

= WINSTON CHURCHILL +

Task Force 135
Veterans' Memories of May 1945

H.R.H. PRINCE CHARLES JOINED THE 50TH LIBERATION CELEBRATIONS, ON MAY 9TH 1995

It is not surprising that many older people like myself (and older), want to write of the war time experiences – especially if being in the forces and having travelled to countries involved in battle. It was just before and after May 9th 1995 and our Liberation celebrations of 50 years, that I received dozens of letters from the veterans of Force 135 – just wanting to remember the special time in Guernsey of 1945. These veterans were given an invitation to the Island and to share with us the big day and appreciated very much the excellent time they had. I feel sure you would be interested in some of their comments.

20th May 1995 from Reg Wickens –

It was really a wonderful time for us all, we will never forget it, All the special arrangements, more food than we could eat, tea, coffee, wine and champagne. The best thing was meeting three of our company for the first time since 1945. (They all spoke on the radio having been presented with a medallion duly inscribed on the back with Force 135 mentioned. They like others were thrilled to have this and were very proud of them.)

Mr Terry Owen writes on 22 March 1995 of his memory of events –

My landing craft assault ship, the *Empire Rapier*, was the first to arrive and my assault craft led the way into the harbour. The German troops were waiting for us and several women holding young children were there – also two Russian Prisoners who were in a sorry state. I gave them a tin of food from our emergency ration box. The rest of it I gave to the woman. We ferried the troops out to our ship and took them to Southampton then returned to Guernsey. After walking around the fort (which the Germans were still guarding) and inspecting some light tanks in a field, we went back to the ship and next day we attended a church service of thanksgiving.

He goes on to say, he volunteered at 17½ in the Royal Marines, passed as a commando and then opted for landing craft and became a stoker/driver, but before he was demobbed at 21 he had seen service and events at the Hong Kong riots and had taken a Pathe news Cameraman round the bows of the Battle ship with Mountbatten entering Singapore for the Jap surrender.

Another letter dated 2nd November 1994. Albert Hall from Bolton, Lancs writes –

> I have many happy memories and many stories that I could tell of my stay in 1945. I claim to have brought the 1st dog to your Island, a fox hound pup that I gave to Mr and Mrs Arthur and Claire Brett of Oceana Cottage, L'Islet. The Brett's named the pup 'Bolton' and I believe he lived to a ripe old age of 15 years.

Mr Hall wanted to resume friendship with these friends of 1945, and hopefully he did.

Part of another letter dated 26 September 1994 from Norman Hannigan:

> Dear Molly,
> Yours is certainly a voice from the past! I have not returned to the Islands since the war but I well remember clearing mines and booby traps from L'Ancresse Bay and its environment. Congratulations to you on surviving five years of German Occupation, your parents must have gone through a mental hell at times, in trying to feed and clothe you children. Any nation that has not been 'occupied' doesn't really know the meaning of war. Enough of this! Live for today and the future, Lass. You seem to be coping very well. God wiling, I will have the pleasure of meeting you next year.

Mr Beresford Winspear (aged 87 in October 1994) wrote and told me that during his stay in Guernsey 1945, he was engaged in arranging an air service with Croydon, England, as this was the airfield used for the daily flights which made a quick return for those English holiday-makers who were unable to return home in 1940! (What a holiday this proved to be!)

George McPherson wrote on October 1994. After receiving my letter, he writes:

> In fact I rarely forget the Island, for on the lounge wall hangs a 15-inch picture of MMS 244 with the coast of St Sampson's in the background. It was taken off a press photo and given to me by the CO a number of years ago. We still keep in contact with one another. The MMS 244 was built in Canada in a little place called Mitagan. We commissioned her there and sailed her to Plymouth, which was our base for three years; then came to Guernsey. As we had not any naval stores in St. Peter Port, being Coxswain, I was given money by the 1st Lieutenant to send some of the lads ashore for stores, may I say there were plenty of volunteers for that duty!

He goes on to say he really enjoyed his time on the Island – he with others were minesweeping around the shores in the day only, (which pleased him) not at night time. He always intended to return for a holiday, but his wife was disabled so was unable to do so – neither could he come for the 50th which was a shame.

Mr J. Clydesdale writes on 25 January 1995. He apparently was evacuated at 13 to Dumfries when the war started, but because his family missed him and his sister so much, they were brought back home. He says later many evacuees from the Channel Islands were brought to Pollokshaws and billeted temporarily in the church hall till homes were found for them in the country. Apparently his mother sent him to invite some of them in for tea. Five or six boys and girls came a few times and they were taken to the local park. He missed his new Guernsey friends after they left as he remembers them being a very cheery crowd.

He continues:

(In 1943 I was now seventeen years old so joined the navy.) I was posted to an ocean going rescue tug, HMRT *Growler*.

> After service in the Atlantic Convoys and Normandy's mulberry harbour we done duty in the English Channel – then came May 9th 1945 where I did end up, Guernsey!
>
> I remember coming ashore in the evening sunshine and in a street near the harbour, a lady invited us into her house for a drink of water. It was probably all she had in the house, she just wanted to say 'Hello' and we shared her happiness. I believe if the house is still there I could go to it yet, there was a small stair outside. Inside one wall was covered in lovely plates, the lady said her daughter had arranged them – I think the daughter had some disability – I did not meet her.
>
> So after all these years since some children from your part of the world came to our house for tea, my wife and myself are having the compliment returned and have been invited to Guernsey to share your Liberation Celebration. How nice. I was only there a short time but remember the shop windows had only goods for barter. The Germans stripped it bare, no doubt about that. However we now look forward to happier times and I wish you a wonderful time on your lovely Island. (PS I wonder if anyone remembers Poloc Church?).

Now Mrs Fay Payne writes of her husband George who had passed away previously in August 1994. She says –

> George loved Guernsey, he was a survivor of HMS *Charybdis* which was sunk in the Channel and some of his ship mates were washed ashore there and buried in Guernsey. We used to come to this event every October years ago. (A commemorative service is held every year for the survivors.)

Then George was on board the HMS *Bulldog* and was in Guernsey in 1945 when the Germans came aboard to sign the surrender of the Channel Islands. All this made him feel very close to your Island. (This is not surprising as these two events were very special during the five years).

Mr J. Clement of Sussex wrote of rather special memories of May 9th –

> I marched the first troops (200 of us) into St. Peters Port on that memorable day, and I shall certainly not forget it. We were very fortunate that the Germans

provided no opposition! We all thought that your Islanders were wonderful to have survived all the hardships of the Occupation which must have been a long dreary anxious five years.

My wife and I are most certainly coming to Guernsey for the Liberation Celebrations. We came for the 40th as we also know Mr and Mrs Richard Heaume quite well.

When writing, Mr Gerry Hussey of Leicester kindly sent me some newspapers as souvenirs as he was afraid they might be thrown away sometime as rubbish. He 'thinks' he landed with his jeep at L'Ancresse Bay on May 10th and drove straight to the Normandy Hotel but stayed only for a couple of weeks. During this short time though, he made many friends and even met up with a Mrs Anne Fox whilst at the celebrations after 50 years! I did try to trace a Mr John Le Moigne for him at the time but without any luck in finding out anything about him.

Stan Crowther of Rotherham wrote (24th October 1994) –

I was a member of a Royal Signals section operating radio teleprinters. It seems a little odd, in the light of modern technology, that that was the first time such equipment had ever been used operationally.

We came ashore somewhere in the south (?) side of the Island after the Royal Engineers had blown a hole in the huge defensive wall which the Germans had erected, and we set up our wireless station in the middle of the night in a field in St. Martins parish. As you probably know, it was just impracticable for the many thousands of German soldiers in Guernsey and Jersey to be disarmed and imprisoned by the very small force 135, and Brigadier Snow had agreed with the German Commander that, as a temporary measure, each Island would simply be divided in two, with the Germans in each Island, confined to one half until things could be sorted out. The only suitable site for our station, from which our aerials could be beamed towards Southern Command HQ at Salisbury, was in the middle of the German half!

Although our equipment had frequently broken down in trials before we got there, we operated without a hitch for six weeks, dealing with war correspondents copy military traffic and hundreds of civilian telegrams.

After being congratulated on their work by Brigadier Snow, we spent another three weeks doing nothing much, but just lounging around on the sunny beaches and enjoying the company of local residents. He continues I am sure none of us felt at all like 'heroes' (we Islanders thought they were!) – the heroes were local people like, for example, a chap called George (I forget his second name) who had been an amateur radio enthusiast before the Occupation and risked deportation by building crystal sets on which his friends listened to the BBC – but it was good to be involved in the Liberation of the only bit of the British Isles occupied by the enemy).

A.E. Priest of Cornwall 'fully remembers' the day they landed at St. Peter Port. He was a member of the DCLI Band and visited all over the Island playing for the Liberation. Later returning to Guernsey they had the job of searching German Officers and ranks before sending them off to England and to prison camps.

Wonderful sounds on the Esplanade (Richard Heaume)

Sydney Sheralt of Cumbria wrote –

Whilst I'm sure no one in this country at the time thought you were having a picnic, I don't think anyone really appreciated the extent of your hardships, the deprivation (and the lack of freedom you endured, all of which you have faithfully recorded in your books. It really is amazing how everyone coped in such circumstances, but when put to the test, there seems no limit to human endurance.

I can well understand the disquiet felt by the Islanders when the whole of Europe was liberated while you were still in chains, but imagine the bloodshed and destruction you would have had to suffer had an earlier attempt been made. It was much more sensible to bring Hitler to his knees, making a much more peaceful Liberation possible.

Tom Birch of Worcester remembers vividly and writes on 11th October 1994 –

(Yes, I do remember Liberation Day on May 9th 1945 as I was one of those who landed at the White Rock at approx 10 am that morning, from an L.C.H. of which also landed 200 soldiers. I was a member of the Royal Navy and landed with two other members. We followed the troops down the White Rock and they went off to the Royal Hotel as we made our way to the Crown Hotel which was our Headquarters, and I naturally remember the gladness and happiness of the people that we met.

He knew Guernsey very well as he eventually married a Guernsey girl (who was a nurse at the Castel Hospital during the Occupation) while still in the Royal Navy.

After being demobbed in 1954, he joined the Island police force until 1979 and then due to family circumstances, returned home. They have returned to the Island since, because they had family still living here.

Now, I must tell you a small part of Mr Ernest Bevin's life. He was born on 24th April 1920 in Nuneaton and I had the pleasure of meeting him at the reception given for the veterans on our 50th Liberation Anniversary. He wrote several times after and finally with many poems, and a book on his life from childhood. I feel sure you might find the last few months of his 'war years' especially interesting. He drove lorries and heavy 'carrier' vehicles and he was trained for bomb disposal. Most of his service during this time was on the continent, he really did have a story to tell (40 full large sheets in fact!). Ernest Bevins ('Bev') tells his story in a light-hearted way but between the lines, one can read of terrible tragedies he witnessed since his joining up in 1940.

He recalls when from Brussels:

Now the order came to try to get to Dunkirk, we were in retreat, everywhere was chaos. We set off, passing through a village, there was shelling all around us. One hit a house and buried me, in the darkness, my mates walked on, thinking I must be gone, but I must have been kicking my legs, when someone pulled me out. A group of guards pulled me free and took me with them. Then an ambulance truck pulled up and offered us a ride for as long as we could go because Jerry was closing in and blocking all the road. So off we went; we stopped, it was daylight; we had been asleep. The driver said we had had a lucky escape; a plane had peppered the truck; our tailboard was in tatters. My! Were we lucky!

Then the sight met our gaze – trucks burning, guns blown up. It meant walking from here. Eventually we got to Dunkirk. There, all hell was raging; the town on fire, lots of boats sunk, thousands of men all along the sands. Diving for cover as another wave of planes peppered the beach. The men dived for cover and it was amazing how many got up after each raid. I thought 'I've heard about hell; this must be it'. How in God's name we survived this long must be a miracle.

On the beaches of La Panne, Dunkirk, we saw another miracle as lots of small boats came from England to help rescue their young men. When we climbed in the boats we were ordered to discard all our equipment, rifles, bullets, tin hats, gas masks, etc to save more men. Men did miracles, picking us up in little boats and taking us to the big ones. I got onto a paddle steamer from the Thames. I think it was *The Royal Eagle* I thought God must be on our side. The sea was like a millpond. Just as well because the boat had many bodies on, more than it should have. I got into a cabin; a sailor brought us tea, biscuits and bully. In a cabin made for six there were eighteen! Then sleep took over.

Hours later, a shout 'England! The White Cliffs!' And the Captain shouting, 'Stand still. You'll turn us over!' Then we pulled into the dock – God must be with us. (Bev was so pleased to be home for a while as he had been injured and gangrene had set in. He was in hospital for a time).

When recovered, Bev then told of his frights, escapes and times when he was scared doing his bomb disposal work all over London, Bristol, Plymouth, Dover and Folkstone. Whilst at Folkstone, they lost a sapper and their officer was very badly injured.

He continues:

D-Day – We had to wait, that's what got us down; we were waiting for D-Day and they wouldn't let us go because there were British people on the Island. Let's face it, they would have wiped them Islands out. We could have stood off the shore and they could have blowed us to pieces and we could have blowed them to pieces, but there would have been nobody left, would there? The Islands would have been sunk, more or less. Although the British troops had gone by and were all up in Belgium and Holland, they still would not surrender. They were nearly starving you know. I'm pretty sure there wasn't a dog or a cat or even a hedgehog or anything on the Island, the Germans had eaten them all.

In the meantime, we kept on with our bomb disposal. We had our laughs. I remember in Dover, his big guns were shelling from Calais and we were in the cliff caves. One old lady came in and said 'I don't think Adolph likes me. Yesterday they got my house, only the outside toilet was left standing and now there's only the hole and the toilet-roll left!' Everyone laughed, though God only knew why.

There were always times one was scared; one's hands were clammy, sweat trickled down one's neck, especially messing with mines or bombs. But you tried to be brave because you know if you started shaking, well, you wouldn't hear the bang!

Once in London, I heard the lads in the back laughing. We asked why. They said the traffic was packing in behind us so they lifted a bomb, a small oil bomb and the board 'Danger Unexploded Bomb'. They said everybody stopped. Suddenly the road was empty. They made their own fun; they had to, one never knew when the ticking might stop. (Nowadays, bomb disposal teams are never allowed to work for more than four months. Bev's team operated for nearly four years, on and off.)

When Churchill broadcast that the war was over, he said to our people in the Channel Islands, help is on the way, this time it was operation Nestegg, 135 Task Force, Liberation of the Channel Islands; ours was Guernsey, we were on the boat then, we thought, well the war is over, so we must be going to Japan or somewhere, and we had a thirty-ton lorry with enough equipment, me and my mate, to light up half of Guernsey, I think. All the men were skilled men like carpenters, plumbers, you name it – yes – big lads. To help put the Island right, you see.

Although the islands were cut off, the Allied armies having captured France, the Commander of the Islands was a top-ranking officer and would not surrender till the top Nazis surrendered, so we sailed over night on VE Day and took over Guernsey the day later. The destroyer, HMS *Bulldog*, went into the harbour, and the Yankie captain on the boat that we were on said, 'signaller, what's that damn light saying?!' He said 'It's the German commander, sir, he says just tell them it's not 12 o'clock; get out or he'll blow you out!' The destroyer went 'Pip-pip-pip', turned round and came out and sat by the entrance just like a cat waiting for a mouse, as soon as it were 12 o'clock he went back in again and then we went – the Engineers. The Germans were sent to the other side of the Island to avoid any clashes with our troops.

Two of our lads had been, and knocked a wall down so that we could get off and put steel wire on the sand. They sent me off first; I was the first lorry off the boat. They said 'Bevins, you go first, you've got 35 tons so if you blow up they'll know we've arrived.' I had got all sandbags around me; I could just move my feet and hands, in case of misdemign. And then our job then was clearing mines that had been missed and God knows what.

The people were near starvation, eating seaweed. I was able to visit some of the Island boys' families (boys whom he had trained at Barnstaple). I enjoyed several months with them. One lady and my wife wrote to each other each Christmas until, sadly, they both passed away, they cooked me some seaweed; 'most horrible'. When we finally landed it was kisses and hugs from the ladies; the men shook hands, patted our backs and asked if we had any cigs. We gave the children sweets – they thought it was Christmas.

The Germans had used slave labour over there. Many died, and the Russian prisoners, we had to de-louse and feed them. Then they were sent to the mainland for hospitalisation. They looked like pictures of the concentration camps and their staring eyes said 'Thank you'. The Germans were all imprisoned and made to work clearing the Island of mines etc. They had still left some booby traps for us.

One thing sticks in my mind. I was standing by my lorry; the lads were clearing out a Jerry store, making sure there were no booby traps, when an old lady came to me – it was lovely weather – with tears in her eyes, and she said, 'There you are. I said an English soldier would have the first strawberry and you're it'. And I had to stand there and eat it, and I cried with her.

The weather was good and a great relief for us to know some of the war was over. Japan was still going. I and my mate found a German staff car, Sunbeam Talbot tourer. We checked it over for booby traps, then used it for ourselves. Then a nice lady said to us it was hers, the Germans had taken it. We said, 'Have you papers of proof?' she had, so we took her to our officer. He handed it over to her, we felt sad at our loss and she also thought Santa Claus had come.

Then after 4½ months getting the Islands habitable, it was time to leave. The troops came on the ferry; me and my mate had to bring our two large lorries back on a LCT, we were tossed about for four days because of stormy weather. Still we didn't mind because Japan had surrendered so it was home on leave, home for Christmas and demob to look forward to, after six and a half years, going home, our jobs done, and thanking God we were still alive.

Ernest Bevins, 'Bev'

Bev wrote this poem following his visit to Guernsey for the Liberation
Celebrations in 1995:

To the Veterans – Who are they?
Yes, we went back to the Islands
Where fifty years ago
We went to free our people
From Hitler's Nazi foe.
Veterans from different units,
It surely made one proud;
Comradeship not forgotten,
Made us want to shout aloud.
My son said 'Dad, the friendship
It really is so grand,
Hard to find it today
Anywhere in the land.'
'No, son, that's for sure',
But they have never stood side by side
To fight a horrible war
The joy the people felt
When they watched us come ashore;
No more tramping Jack boots,
No knocks upon the door.
Now they could sleep solidly for sure,
For at last they were free again,
No fears, no more war.

They paid for us to join them,
Join them in their fun,
But this time 'Wear your medals,
Leave behind your gun'
What a wonderful time they gave us,
Wine and food and more,
Just to thank us for what we did
That day we came ashore.
We got rid of the Nazis,
Set the prisoners free;
Then put the islands back to rights,
The veterans and me.
So thank you, kindly people,
For all your hospitality.
May God bless you all,
From the veterans and me.

Bev also has written many letters and in one he said –

When I was on your lovely Island I had POWs working for me clearing mines etc. one young German boy carved me a lovely rose or fruit bowl. Really beautiful it was, but when I brought my lorry back with lots of gifts for the lads, some one kindly stole it! Still that's another story.

Bev's memory was certainly marvellous and throughout his book he sounded a wonderful character, I only met him for a short time but his letters were always very warm and friendly to me. With his very first memories he wrote –

I came off that huge boat, (doors opening in the front) and came along the sea front, then up the main street to a huge garage where we left the lorries, mine was 35 tons. Full of machinery to help put the Island back to rights. We were told to drive on the right, but a Red Cap (military police) told me to go over to the left side. Then that welcome, I'll never forget it, wonderful kisses and hugs and the children's faces when we gave them some sweets, I'll never forget those memories.

What really made a lump come in my throat was when I had people come to shake hands and say 'Thank you', 'Well done' especially children.

I sat in the square in St Peter Port and a small girl came up with her parents and said, could she look at my medals? I said, 'Yes, would you like to touch them?' she said 'Please, oh aren't they heavy, you are very nice thank you for saving us' and her parents shook my hand and said 'thanks' that's when the tears came. (Lovely memories.)

14th May 1995 Mr Ernest Bevins (Bev) tells me he wrote to Major Evan Ozanne and the Tourist board and gave thanks for giving him such a wonderful time, quote – I'm sure all of 135 Task Force thank you for the most wonderful and memorable time over on your lovely Island that your good people gave us. Really really grand. I'm sure not one man of us will ever forget. The 'Cavalcade' well, no words can describe it, MARVELLOUS. People must have put lots of hard work into it and the medallion you gave us 'BEAUTIFUL'. Everyone was proud of it. Better than the ones we got for 'fighting' the war. How can anyone of us ever repay you all. Really warm and loving three days with some wonderful people.

Again on the next letter thanking everyone who gave Force 135 veterans a 'wonderful, wonderful' time and apparently on the way home on the Condor, they were all 'full of it' and so proud of their beautiful medals. (Reading his account of war makes me realise all these veterans have stories and many brave times we shall never know about.)

On the 16th May 1997, Bill Smith from Lancashire, another veteran, wrote:

I received my book from you and I must express my thanks and gratitude for the kind letter you wrote. It will always be one of my prize possessions and I've read it four times since I received it. Thank you for writing it, it's wonderful. I have spoken to 'Bev' and passed on your good wishes. I now have a request I wish you to do for me.

When I landed in St. Peter Port on my LCA from my parent ship in 1945 to sort out the German troops and load up with them as POWs to bring back to Southampton, I took chocolate and cigarettes and all good things to give to our people. As you now know, the welcome we got was unbelievable and as a young 19-year-old Royal Marine, the tears flowed without any embarrassment and I gave some cigs and chocolate to an old gentleman who hugged me and said 'Thank God you have arrived.' He then gave me a folded up piece of paper and said 'There is a souvenir for you son.' I didn't have time to read it and placed it in my Battle Dress top pocket and got on with the job in hand – later that day, after ferrying loads of P.O.Ws, I was feeling in my pocket and found the piece of paper. I opened it up and found it to be a leaflet with photographs of the burial of Naval ratings which were washed up on the beaches from the HMS *Charybdis*. I have kept this brochure for over 50 years now and it is one of my best remembrance items that I have.

Now when I returned for your 50th Celebrations, I vowed that I would find the graves of these young naval ratings and pay them my respect. After we had been presented with our Guernsey Liberation medals, I met one of the veterans who was staying with me at the Peninsula Hotel and told him of my intentions.

The long letter continues to say together with the new veteran friends (Mr and Mrs George Cox from Suffolk) that they all paid their respect to the Naval ratings and Mr Smith and Mr Cox both had photographs taken saluting the graves at the Foulon Cemetery where these well kept graves are. Bill Smith just asked me to forward a book to these good people, as he did enjoy their company.

Stanley Templeman from Shropshire was another who kept in touch for a long time. On the 26th November 1995, he writes:

Yes, at last, we have received our commemorative Liberation medal. I think it's a splendid medal and I will wear it with pride on comrades reunions and other such parades where medals are worn.

Major Evan Ozanne took on a mamouth task when trying to trace veterans of the Task Force 135 to invite them all to the Island to join in our celebrations and to receive the medal in gratitude and appreciation of their time here and to celebrate with us the 50 years of freedom. It was Guernsey's way of saying 'thank you' for their war effort in bringing us our liberation.

The search was made in many parts of the world and many veterans accepted but some were unable to accept the invitation for different reasons, mainly age and illnesses. The ones that could not travel did not lose out on receiving their medal, the gift from the States of Guernsey, as they were presented with them in many towns and cities all over the mainland and beyond.

In the photograph overleaf, these veterans were presented with their 'special' medal by the Lord Mayor in Birmingham.

Although I had received many other letters from all basically expressing their thanks, I was also pleased to receive a very nice letter from a Mr Derek Sprake who had travelled from the Isle of Wight especially for the celebrations – he was not disappointed! He begins:

Left to right: *Ronald Wells, Stanley Templeman, Cliff Skidmore, Ralph Field, Alfred Farme and Lord Mayor David Roy*

Dear Molly, Having returned home after having spent the most wonderful and moving few days of my life on your Island, I felt I just had to write and thank you, firstly for suggesting my stay at Les Cotils, and through you, to the Island of Guernsey for a superb Liberation Day.

He remarked how everyone was so kind and friendly and he was thrilled to have the most perfect position to see Prince Charles and everything else going on. Prince Charles evidently came and stood talking to them and to others outside the Concourse Entrance. He felt sorry for several short people who stood behind him, and also a partially blind young man who asked what was going on. He more or less did a commentary for one and all after that.

Now in his words:

What a simply wonderful day, what a wonderful occasion, what a wonderful event – a day I will treasure in my mind forever. It was an honour to be there, although perhaps I felt, just for a moment, that I should not be there – it was Guernsey peoples day and not mine. So many happy people just enjoying themselves.

And then that wonderful Cavalcade. We just happened to be stood with Deputy Tony Webber, his family and aunt, she gave us a lovely description of her Liberation Day.

As she said, 'I kissed so many soldiers that day.' There were tears of joy in her eyes. And so it went on; the Red Arrows were great, and all the other aircraft. What a shame it all had to end.

When we left Les Cotils, a lady who was also staying there was stood outside. She was almost in tears, she lives in England, was born in Guernsey and lived there until 17 years ago. She said she was heartbroken at the thought of going back her home and her heart was still in Guernsey, she has lost her husband and there is nothing to stop her returning to live there, except that she has a disabled daughter and she feels she cannot leave her in England or bring her to Guernsey.

And as to the monument itself, I listened to all the talk about it on the radio, to the States debates on it, I saw the model in the foyer of the Royal Court, I made a small donation towards it, I saw it covered in plastic, I saw it covered in our flag, and I saw the shadow fall exactly on the correct spot as the sun moved round. I saw the Prince of Wales unveil it, I think it is superb, a simple and unique memorial quite different from anything else and a fitting tribute to that special day in your history. And so its all over, but as I wait for my numerous photographs to return, I can look back and say 'I was there.' Thank you Guernsey.

With every good wish & many thanks,
Derek Sprake
May 1995

Some members of Task Force 135. Many from this photo taken on 4th October 1945 were made to feel welcome at our home

German troops awaiting transport to POW camps after Liberation

The 40th, 50th and 60th Anniversaries of the Liberation Celebrations

40TH ANNIVERSARY OF LIBERATION

Guernsey has always celebrated Liberation during the month of May and until fairly recently celebrated on the nearest Wednesday (the original week day when Liberation occurred) to 9th May, with always a special thanksgiving church service every year. As early as 1946 there was a calvacade and in 1947, '48, '49, '50, again in 1951. There were no calvacades again until 1975 but every five years since there has been every effort to celebrate in this way.

THE BRITISH LIBERATING FORCES
LANDED ON THIS SLIPWAY
ON THE 9th MAY 1945
AND
THIS STONE WAS UNVEILED BY
HER ROYAL HIGHNESS THE DUCHESS OF KENT
ON THE 9th MAY 1985 TO COMMEMORATE
THE 40th ANNIVERSARY
OF THE ISLAND'S LIBERATION

The 40th Anniversary was a very special day and occasion, as Her Royal Highness The Duchess of Kent unveiled this stone near the slipway where the British Liberating Forces landed the trucks and different vehicles and materials etc and many of the Force 135 came ashore. It was at this area I clearly remember this tall 'posh' city gent arrived off the large landing craft walking across the sand firmly holding his bowler on his head, clutching a despatch case and a rolled up umbrella – it was a strange sight to see such an important man in a smart dark suit coming towards us. Everyone cheered and sang 'There'll always be an England'. Later it was reported on the English newspaper that he was Mr C.D. Brickmore, a civil servant from London, who was carrying very important plans for the complete rehabilitation of the Island. He certainly had the loudest cheer of the day and what a sight for us who were there – 12th May 1945.

50TH ANNIVERSARY OF LIBERATON

Artist Eric Snell (a Guernseyman) was commissioned by the States of Guernsey to design a monument to commemorate the 50th Anniversary of the Islanders liberation. The monument is precisely placed to mark the path of the sun on the 9th May 1945. This tip of the shadow of the 5 metre obelisk falls on a curve of stone seating throughout the day and provides a link between 1945, 1995 and on each Liberation Day in the future. Inscriptions on the seating record the major events of the 9th May 1945 as read.

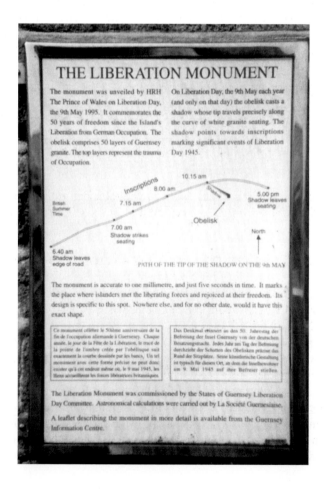

The signing of the surrender of the German Forces at 7.15am. The landing of the British liberation Force at 8am. The unfurling of the Union flag at 10.15am. Also recorded is Winston Churchill's memorable statement – 'Our dear Channel Islands are also to be freed today'. At the east end of the seating the words 'Thanks be to God' are inscribed in English and Guernsey French. HRH the Prince of Wales visited the Island and military presence included – The Band of HM Royal Marines, HMS Norfolk, Band of the Royal Artillery, Colour Party and Guard 201 Squadron (RAF Kinloss), Battle of Britain Memorial Flight and the Red Arrows.

There was a 21 gun salute at Castle Cornet and after a parade Inspection the inauguration of the 50th Anniversary Memorial obelisk by HRH the Prince of Wales took place.

His message to the island was:

> Almost 55 years ago the Channel Islands became the only part of the British Empire to be subject to German Occupation. 50 years after their liberation I am enormously proud to be with you to help celebrate that historic event.
>
> I have heard much of the hardships and sufferings endured by those Islanders who remained during the occupation and also of those who were separated from their families, whether as members of the forces, or as deportees and evacuees. There is no doubt that the traditional island qualities of independance and determination which carried you through the long and difficult war years remain undiminished by time.
>
> It gives me great pleasure to be able to join the people of Guernsey in celebrating half a century of freedom, liberty and prosperity and to share with you all the joys of this significant and special anniversary.
>
> Signed Charles

The 50th celebration was a very special memorable day with a spectacular calvacade and firework display and was enjoyed by thousands, in glorious weather.

60TH ANNIVERSARY OF OUR LIBERATION, 9TH MAY 2005

I joined a group of Guernsey friends for the large cavalcade for the 55th Anniversary and walked from the Salarie Corner, they could remember our Liberation Day and what it meant to each one of us. Our thoughts are always with our families at this time, who sadly have passed away, whilst some other parents are very elderly now and cannot enjoy the day. One such lady I walked with was Rosemary McClean (nee Savident) and her husband Brian. Speaking to her recently, she said that she intends to walk in the parade again this year – really to emphasise the importance of remembering (especially) our mothers during the war years and how they had to cope and go without for us children. Rosemary was born on 3rd March 1942 and her mother was taken by horse ambulance for the birth at the Castel Hospital.

Her mother, Mona (nee Frampton) was poorly in health and weighed only six stone at this time. She was also caring for her mother who had heart disease and early in 1945, another daughter Ann was born.

Although very young, Rosemary clearly remembers being frightened for her mother when one day the Germans had called at the house and found coal which her father, Wilfred (a fisherman) had brought home and shouldn't have. The German was angry and smacked her mother across the face and little Rosemary screamed 'Leave my mummy alone!' This fear has stayed with Rosemary and whilst visiting Israel in 1985 with a Christian group on holiday, she froze and couldn't move when seeing a group of soldiers with guns. The memory of that incident came back to her. Likewise, of a friend of mine who remembers a German Officer asking him a question in school (to be answered correctly!) and how frightened he felt, even to this day.

As we walked we remembered our dear parents and loved ones and the sacrifice they all made. We payed tribute to them then, and grateful for our freedom and peaceful years we have enjoyed since.

Despite the laughter and fun we all share when Liberation Day comes around, we (who remember) do feel emotional remembering that very special time of our lives and I don't think we shall ever forget Liberation Day.

For the 60th celebration the weather was perfect, a glorious day with a clear blue sky and just as I remember 9th May 1945. Her Majesty Queen Elizabeth and His Royal Highness the Duke of Edinburgh were to make a visit for the special occasion.

Liberation celebrations began well before the great day, all over the Island. On the 5th May there was a concert held of 'Liberated Youth' a unique concert for the younger generation which was an evening of music, dance and drama. Three films were shown, the first was *Nazi Britain*, telling of Islanders who lived through the occupation – the second was *Stolen by Hitler*, accounts of British men, women and children who were deported to Germany and finally *Fleeing the Reich* – Islanders who evacuated during June 1940 and telling of their separation from loved ones for 5 years and how this affected them. The trilogy of films were made by Martin Morgan, deputy head of programming for the History Channel.

Children in schools were having special 'war' lessons before and after liberation day and expressing what war and occupation would have been like to them. Many tea parties were also being enjoyed. A party tea dance and a sing-song for some 750 World War Two Islanders and veterans enjoyed a wonderful afternoon. A lovely atmosphere amongst old friends has become an annual event and looked forward to. Many events and also street entertainment etc to suit all ages are kindly sponsored by many, to give everyone enjoyment.

Her Majesty the Queen and His Royal Highness the Duke of Edinburgh duly arrived in the morning to be greeted by the Governor, Bailiff and Dignitaries, and hundreds of school children and Islanders at the Airport, and along the route to Beau Sejour, where they joined over 1000 people for a thanksgiving and reconciliation service. Many

The Queen unveiling the commemoration plaque, 9th May 2005

WINDSOR CASTLE

8th April, 2005

Dear Mrs. Bihet,

    The Queen wishes me to write and thank you for your letter, and for your kindness in enclosing a copy of your memoirs on the Occupation of Guernsey from 1940 to 1945.

    Her Majesty received this with great pleasure and was touched by your personal recollections of the Liberation Day. The Queen hopes to have read your book before her visit to Guernsey on 9th May, a visit to which Her Majesty is greatly looking forward.

    The Queen much appreciated the sentiments expressed in your letter, and I am to thank you again for your thoughtful gift.

Yours sincerely,

Mary Henderson

Lady-in-Waiting

Mrs. M. Bihet

veterans of World War Two were present and from Task Force 135 (the liberation force) when some made the effort to join us. I felt very proud as our two grandchildren Naomi and Joshua Cottam were playing in the Guernsey Youth Orchestra at the service. Naomi playing cello and Josh playing percussion. The Salvation Army Band also played and the Guernsey Girls Choir also sang.

During the early afternoon, everybody who had worked hard in numerous ways were ready for the procession and calvacade that we were all looking forward to. No one was disappointed and over 2000 children and adults took part. Music, horses, bicycles, decorated vehicles, World War Two vehicles and pre-1945 vintage cars etc etc, all paraded along the seafront, with entertainment all around. Again, Josh was playing percussion with Eight in a Bar, a popular jazz band, during the afternoon. They also played at our Golden Anniversary dance that we celebrated in December 2004 and they helped to make it a most enjoyable evening.

Back to the 60th celebrations, everyone had a wonderful day and throughout the evening. At 10pm the day finished with a glorious firework display from Castle Cornet. I hope like many others Liberation Day will never be forgotten and will always be remembered as Guernsey's Special Day, as it has been since 9th May 1945 when we were so thankful once again for our Freedom.

When knowing the Queen and Prince Philip had accepted the invitation to visit Guernsey, I decided to send the Queen my book *A Child's War*. I was thrilled to receive a letter from her lady-in-waiting with a thank you from the Queen (opposite). I shall never know if Her Majesty did get to read of my family's occupation, I do hope so, however, I did later receive a letter from Buckingham Palace saying how much they enjoyed their visit to Guernsey.

Myself facing (in the centre) with other excited Islanders greeting the first troops (artillerymen) to land at the harbour on the morning of 9th May 1945. Their fixed bayonets can be seen. (Grateful thanks to Mr Bill Bell and the Guernsey Archives for allowing me to reproduce this photograph

Seated at the Monument (February 2005) where I can still recall and see clearly those first British soldiers marching up the harbour. Those 22 men were such a lovely sight and we felt so grateful. We, the hundred or so Islanders who had gathered early in the morning, just had to run and greet them and to thank them.

The monument designed by Mr Eric Snell to commemorate the 50th anniversary of the liberation

At long last, especially to our beloved parents and grandparents, everyone could again be free. It is a date to be remembered and one which will certainly go down in Guernsey's history books.

Further Reading

A Child's War – Molly Bihet
Amberley Publishing, 2009

ISBN 978-1-84868-205-4

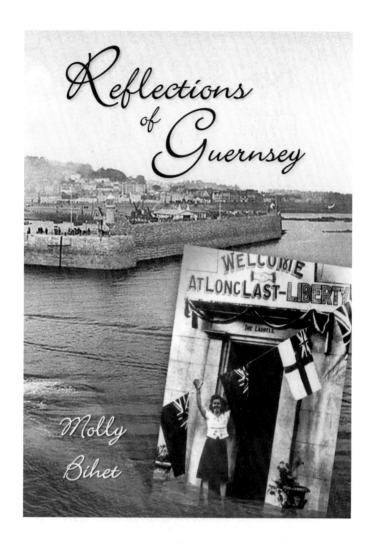

Reflections of Guernsey – Molly Bihet
Amberley Publishing, 2009

ISBN 978-1-84868-206-1

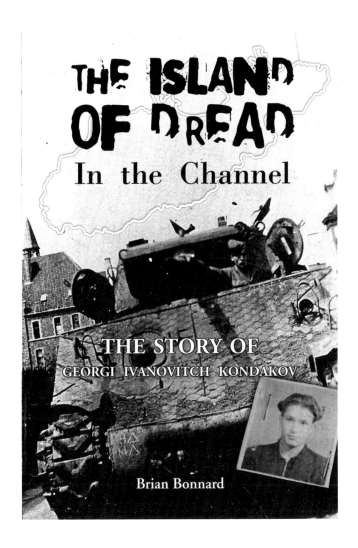

The Island of Dread in the Channel – Brian Bonnard

Amberley Publishing, 2009

ISBN 978-1-84868-361-7

BRIAN BONNARD

ALDERNEY
From Old Photographs

Alderney From Old Photographs – Brian Bonnard
Amberley Publishing, 2009

ISBN 978-1-84868-360-0

Available from all good bookshops, online or direct from:

Amberley Publishing
Cirencester Road
Chalford
Stroud
GL6 8PE